Good Girl, Be BAD

Erica Perry Briody

Published by Good Girl, Be BAD LLC

First Edition

ISBN: 979-8-89864-017-0

For information about special discounts for bulk purchases, please contact Good Girl, Be BAD LLC at info@bebadclub.com

www.bebadclub.com

Dedication

For my daughters, Ashley and Emma—you are my heartbeat, my courage, and my "why."

Every page of this book is woven with the hope that you, and women everywhere, will never shrink from who you are or what you are meant to become.

May you always be bold enough to dream, ambitious enough to chase those dreams, and determined enough to see them through.

This book is my gift to you, and my promise: that you will never walk this journey alone.

With all my love,

Mum.

Acknowledgement

Writing Good Girl, Be BAD has been a journey of courage, perseverance, and love. I am deeply indebted to the remarkable team at Donahue Publishing, whose steadfast belief and expert guidance transformed a dream into reality.

To Brooke—your quiet companionship during countless hours of writing was a gift beyond measure. You were the calm beside me, the gentle encouragement when words felt heavy, and the reminder that I was never alone on this path.

To Monika—your creativity breathed life into the Be BAD Club. Thank you for seeing the vision with me, for shaping its edges, and for daring to believe in its power.

And to my daughters, Ashley and Emma—you are my daily wellspring of strength and inspiration. You are the reason I chose to be bold, ambitious, and determined. This book is my gift to you, as much as it is to every woman who reads it.

With abiding gratitude,

Erica.

Contents

Chapter 1
Be Bold

The phone call came at 8:47 PM on a Tuesday.

I was reviewing resumes for a VP position at our London office when my phone buzzed. The name on the screen made me smile: Sofia, one of my former mentees from São Paulo, now a director at a major tech company.

"Erica," she said, her voice shaking with excitement, "I got the promotion. Senior Director of Global Operations. They said what sealed it was how I handled the board presentation last month—how confident and clear I was."

I remembered that board presentation. Three months earlier, Sofia had called me in tears. "I can't do this," she said. "What if I mess up? What if they think I don't belong in that room?"

But she did it. She walked into that boardroom, presented her strategy for expanding into three new markets, and answered every challenging question with authority.

Here's what Sofia learned—and what every successful woman I've mentored across five continents eventually discovers: boldness isn't a personality trait you're born with. It's a skill you can develop, practice, and master.

Being bold means having the courage to take risks, speak your mind, and step out of your comfort zone. It's about making your presence known and not being afraid to go after what you want. In today's world, being bold sets you apart from the crowd and propels you toward success.

But here's the secret most career advice won't tell you: there's a difference between being bold, being reckless, and being obnoxious. Understanding that difference will change everything about how you show up in the world.

Being reckless means acting without thinking through consequences. Being obnoxious means demanding attention without adding value. Being bold means speaking up strategically, taking calculated risks, and advocating for yourself and others with purpose.

The women who change the world aren't the loudest ones in the room. They're the ones who know when to speak, how to speak, and what's worth speaking up for.

When Silence Costs More Than Speaking Up

Let me tell you about Mia, a young woman I met during a college speaking event in Chicago. After my presentation, she approached me with tears in her eyes.

"I wish I'd heard this two months ago," she said. "I had the perfect solution for our team project, but I kept quiet because I didn't want to seem pushy. We ended up failing because no one spoke up about the obvious problems."

Mia's story isn't unusual. In my years mentoring young professionals, I've heard this same regret countless times: "I knew what to say, but I didn't say it."

The next semester, Mia enrolled in a debate class. Her heart pounded so hard during her first presentation that she thought everyone could hear it. But she remembered our conversation. She stood up, shared her point of view clearly and confidently, and won the round.

Later, she told me: "I realized that staying small wasn't protecting anyone—it was just wasting my ideas."

Sometimes, the boldest thing you can do is open your mouth when every part of you wants to stay silent.

But before we go further, I want you to think about your own relationship with boldness. What's your Mia moment? When did staying quiet cost you something important—an opportunity, a friendship, respect, or just peace of mind?

Here's what I've learned from mentoring hundreds of young women: we all have a voice. The question isn't whether you have something valuable to say. The question is whether you'll trust yourself enough to say it.

The Anatomy of a Bold Move

Real boldness isn't about grand gestures or dramatic moments. It's about small, strategic choices that compound over time. It's about speaking up in meetings when you have a better idea. It's about applying for opportunities even when you don't meet every qualification. It's about having difficult conversations instead of hoping problems will resolve themselves.

Let me show you what this looks like in practice.

Three Bold Strategies That Actually Work

I've tested these strategies across cultures, industries, and career stages. They work because they're based on a simple principle: boldness with purpose gets results.

1. Speak Up Strategically—Not Just Loudly

Last year, I was facilitating a strategy meeting for a marketing team in Mumbai. Twenty minutes in, I noticed one team member—Priya, a junior analyst—shifting in her seat every time the conversation hit a dead end. She clearly had something to say but kept hesitating.

Finally, during a particularly tense moment when the team was stuck on budget allocation, I asked directly: "Priya, what are you thinking?"

She took a breath and said, "I've been analyzing our competitor's campaigns, and I think we're missing a huge opportunity with micro-influencers. The data shows..."

Her insight completely shifted the strategy. The campaign she proposed ended up exceeding targets by 40%.

After the meeting, I asked Priya why she'd waited so long to speak. "I thought maybe I was wrong," she said. "I'm just an analyst."

Here's what I told her—and what I'm telling you: when you have valuable input, staying quiet isn't humble. It's wasteful.

The key is framing your contributions strategically. Instead of saying "This might be wrong, but..." try "I have a suggestion that could improve this project." Instead of "Sorry, but..." try

"Here's another perspective." You're not apologizing for taking up space—you're adding value.

2. Raise Your Hand When You're 70% Ready

When I was building my first international recruitment team, I had a choice to make. We needed someone to lead our expansion into the South African market. I had two candidates: James, who had all the traditional qualifications but was hesitant to take on the challenge, and Sarah, who had 70% of the experience but was eager to learn the rest.

I chose Sarah.

Why? Because in my experience across five continents, the people who succeed aren't the ones who wait until they feel 100% ready. They're the ones who raise their hand when they're 70% prepared and figure out the rest through action.

Sarah didn't just succeed—she built the most profitable division in our company's history.

Here's the truth about readiness: if you wait until you feel completely qualified, someone else will already have the job. The gap between 70% ready and 100% ready is usually just confidence, not competence.

Look for leadership opportunities now. Run for student council. Volunteer to manage that group project. Start a club if one doesn't exist for your interests. Each time you lead—even imperfectly—you're building evidence that you can handle bigger challenges.

4

3. Ask for What You Want—Without Apologizing

I learned this lesson the hard way.

Early in my career, I was managing talent acquisition for a growing tech company. I'd successfully filled thirty critical positions in six months, well above target. I knew I deserved a promotion, but I kept waiting for my boss to notice.

Months passed. Nothing.

Finally, a mentor told me something that changed my approach forever: "Erica, your good work speaks for you, but it doesn't speak up for you. That's your job."

I scheduled a meeting with my boss, prepared a clear case showing my impact, and asked directly for the promotion I'd earned. I got it—plus a salary increase I hadn't even thought to request.

Since then, I've coached hundreds of women through similar conversations. The ones who succeed understand this: asking for what you deserve isn't aggressive—it's professional.

Don't apologize for wanting more. Whether it's a raise, a promotion, or the chance to work on an exciting project, prepare your case and ask clearly.

Here's something most people don't know: many managers expect you to negotiate. When you don't, they sometimes assume you don't understand your own value. Don't let that assumption limit your growth.

The Ripple Effect of Bold Choices

Here's what I've observed mentoring young women across different cultures and industries:

boldness creates momentum. One strategic bold move leads to another opportunity, which leads to increased confidence, which leads to bigger bold moves.

Take Sofia, the woman I mentioned at the beginning of this chapter. Her journey to that board presentation didn't start there. It started two years earlier when she spoke up in a team meeting about a process inefficiency. That led to her being asked to join a cross-functional task force. That experience gave her the confidence to volunteer for a high-visibility project. Each bold step prepared her for the next one.

The same pattern works for everyone. You don't start by giving keynote speeches at international conferences. You start by asking a thoughtful question in class. You don't begin by negotiating six-figure salaries. You start by advocating for a small budget increase for your student organization.

Every bold action—no matter how small—is practice for the bigger bold moves your future self will need to make.

Your First Bold Move

Right now, I want you to identify one situation where you've been staying quiet when you should speak up. Maybe it's a group project where you have a better approach. Maybe it's a part-time job where you've noticed an inefficiency. Maybe it's a friendship where you need to address something that's been bothering you.

Choose something that matters but feels manageable. Something that would make a positive difference if you acted on it.

Now, make a plan. When will you speak up? How will you frame your input? What's the worst thing that could realistically happen? What's the best thing that could happen?

Most importantly: what's the cost of continuing to stay silent?

Here's what I know from years of experience: the regret of not speaking up almost always outweighs the temporary discomfort of speaking up.

Building Your Bold Foundation

Throughout this book, we're going to build on this foundation of strategic boldness. In the coming chapters, you'll learn how to be ambitious without being ruthless, how to be determined without being inflexible, and how to integrate all of these qualities into a career strategy that reflects your values and goals.

But it all starts here, with the decision to trust your voice.

The women who change industries, lead organizations, and create positive change in the world all started with one thing: the belief that their voice mattered.

Your voice matters too.

The question isn't whether you have something valuable to contribute. You do.

The question is: are you bold enough to let the world hear it?

What Bold Looks Like for You

Your bold journey won't look exactly like Sofia's or Priya's or mine. Maybe your first bold move is asking a question in your next class. Maybe it's applying for a leadership position in a student organization. Maybe it's having an honest conversation with someone who's been taking advantage of your kindness.

The specific action doesn't matter. What matters is taking that first step.

Here's what I want you to remember: being bold isn't about becoming someone you're not. It's about becoming more fully who you already are. It's about trusting that your ideas, your perspective, and your voice have value.

Because they do.

A Lesson in Standing Up

I want to end this chapter by sharing a story that shaped how I think about boldness—not because it was particularly dramatic, but because it taught me that sometimes the most important bold moves happen in the smallest moments.

In eighth grade, I was part of our school's Battle of the Books team, competing nationally in literature trivia. Our teacher announced that whoever answered the most questions correctly during practice would become team captain—a role that included representing us on television.

After weeks of intense studying, the results were in: I tied with one of the boys on the team. But when it came time to name the captain, my teacher chose him instead. "It will look stronger on television," she said.

My heart sank. I had worked just as hard, memorized just as many books. But at that moment, I had a choice: accept the unfair decision or speak up.

I raised my hand. "Miss Cook, we're tied. I want to challenge him to a final round—ten questions. Whoever gets more right becomes captain."

The room grew quiet. A few teammates snickered. But something inside me refused to back down.

"Fine," I said. "Give me the ten hardest questions. If I get every one right, I've earned the right to be captain."

Ten questions. Ten perfect answers.

That day, I didn't just win a competition. I learned that being bold isn't about being the loudest person in the room. It's about believing in your worth enough to advocate for yourself, even when it's uncomfortable.

I went on to lead our team to victory on television. More importantly, I learned that speaking up for fairness—for myself and others—wasn't selfish or pushy. It was necessary.

Your Bold Future Starts Now

Throughout this book, we're going to build on this foundation of strategic boldness. In Chapter 4, you'll learn how to channel this bold energy into ambitious goal-setting. In Chapter 5, we'll explore how to pair boldness with determination to overcome obstacles and setbacks.

But everything begins here, with the understanding that your voice has value and your ideas deserve to be heard.

The women who change industries, lead organizations, and create lasting impact all started with the same realization: they stopped waiting for permission to contribute and started giving themselves permission to lead.

Your bold journey begins with a single question: What's the first bold step you're going to take?

Don't wait for tomorrow. Don't wait until you feel ready. Don't wait for the perfect moment.

The world needs what you have to offer. It's time to be bold enough to share it.

Chapter 2
The Invitation

The email arrived on a Monday morning, and it changed everything.

Marcus, a talented 22-year-old designer I'd been mentoring, had applied for his dream internship at a prestigious creative agency in New York. His portfolio was impressive, his interview had gone well, and the hiring manager seemed genuinely excited about his potential.

Then came the background check.

"Erica," Marcus said when he called me, his voice shaking, "they rescinded the offer. They said after reviewing my 'online presence,' they didn't think I was a good cultural fit for their team."

What had they found? Nothing scandalous. No inappropriate photos or offensive comments. Just... nothing professional. His social media presence told the story of a college student who liked to party, not a serious creative professional ready to contribute to high-stakes projects.

"I thought my portfolio would speak for itself," he said. "I never realized they'd care about my Instagram posts from two years ago."

Marcus learned a lesson that I wish I could teach every young professional before they need it: in today's world, your digital presence isn't separate from your professional reputation. It is your professional reputation.

The Story You're Already Telling

Here's something most career advice won't tell you: you already have a personal brand. Whether you've intentionally built one or not, every Google search result, every social media post, every photo you're tagged in is telling a story about who you are and where you're headed.

The question isn't whether you have a digital footprint—you do. The question is whether you're in control of the story it's telling.

Your digital footprint refers to the collection of all the information and data you leave behind as you use the internet.

Think of your online presence like this: it's the first impression you make before you even walk into the room. Every photo you post, comment you make, and profile you create is telling a story about who you are and where you're headed.

Most young professionals think about their digital presence only when they're actively job searching. But here's what I've learned from helping hundreds of people navigate career transitions across different industries: the time to build your professional brand is before you need it, not after.

Think of it like a trail of glitter you're leaving behind as you move through the internet. Some of it is beautiful and sparkly. You may wish you could sweep up some of it later.

The Two Stories You're Telling Online

There are two kinds of footprints you leave behind:

- **Active Digital Footprint:** These choices you make on purpose—like posting a photo, sharing your work, or creating a profile that shows the professional person you are. → *This is the story you choose to tell.*

- **Passive Digital Footprint:** These are the traces you leave without realizing it, such as when a website tracks what you look at or when a friend tags you in a photo without your permission. → *This is the part of the story written without your permission.*

The most successful young professionals I've mentored understand something crucial: they don't wait for others to define their online story. They take control of it.

Why This Matters More Than You Think

Here's the reality that Marcus learned too late: before your dream internship interview, before that scholarship committee meets you, before your future boss shakes your hand—they Google you.

What they find in those first few search results can open doors or quietly close them before you even know they existed.

I've been on both sides of this equation. As someone who's hired hundreds of people across different countries, I can tell you that 87% of recruiters and hiring managers look up candidates online. We're not looking for reasons to reject you—we're looking for reasons to get excited about you.

When I Google a candidate and find a thoughtfully curated LinkedIn profile, a portfolio showcasing their work, or evidence of their involvement in causes they care about, it tells me they take their professional development seriously. It shows they understand that success in today's world requires intentional personal branding.

When I find nothing professional at all, or worse, content that contradicts the professional image they're trying to project in interviews, it raises questions about their judgment and self-awareness.

Your digital story today becomes your professional reputation tomorrow. Make it count.

The Google Test: What Story Are You Telling?

Before we talk about building your brand, let's assess what's already out there. I call this the Google Test, and I recommend every young professional do it quarterly.

Here's how it works:

Right now—before you read another word—open a new browser window and search for yourself the way a hiring manager would:

1. Google your full name + your city

2. Search your full name + your school or current employer

3. Search your most-used usernames across platforms

4. Check Google Images for your name

Look at the first two pages of results. What story do they tell? If you were a hiring manager who knew nothing about you except what appeared in these search results, what would you conclude about this person's:

- Professionalism

- Interests and values

- Communication skills

- Readiness for new opportunities

Be honest. Would you want to interview this person? Would you trust them with important projects? Would you feel confident introducing them to clients or senior leadership?

If your answer is anything other than "absolutely yes," then this chapter is going to change your career trajectory.

The AMP Framework: Taking Control of Your Digital Story

After Marcus's experience, I developed a simple system that I've now taught to hundreds of young professionals. I call it the AMP framework, and it's designed to help you take control of your digital narrative strategically and authentically.

You have more power over your professional reputation than you think. You don't have to wait for permission to start building the career you want—you can start today, right from your laptop.

I use three simple letters to help my mentees remember this process: A.M.P.

A — Assess

Start with an honest assessment of what's already out there:

- Google your name, your usernames, and your images.

- See what information, pictures, and comments come up.

Ask yourself: "If a hiring manager spent five minutes googling me right now, what impression would they form?"

But don't stop there. Also consider:

- What platforms are you currently on, and what story does each one tell?

- What photos are you tagged in that you didn't post yourself?

- What comes up when you search for your email address or phone number?

- Are there old accounts or usernames that no longer represent who you are?

→ You can't improve what you don't measure. Get clear on your starting point.

M — Manage

Next, actively manage your existing digital presence:

- Delete old posts and accounts you don't need anymore.

- Reach out to friends about untagging you from content that doesn't align with your professional goals.

- Set your privacy controls so you decide who sees what.

Here's where most people stop, but management goes deeper than just deleting embarrassing photos:

- Update privacy settings on all platforms (and check them regularly—platforms change their policies frequently)

14

- Create a consistent username across professional platforms

- Ensure your profile photos across platforms are appropriate and consistent

- Review and update your bio/about sections to reflect your current goals

→ You're the editor of your digital story. Edit strategically.

P — Promote

Finally, proactively promote your professional brand:

- Share content that showcases your talents, interests, and professional growth.

- Create a LinkedIn profile that positions you for future opportunities. (We'll dive deep into LinkedIn strategy in Chapter 8.)

- Document your achievements, projects, and learning journey. Let people see your growth and potential.

Strategic promotion means:

- Sharing insights from books you're reading in your field

- Posting about projects you're working on (with appropriate discretion)

- Engaging thoughtfully with industry content and conversations

- Showcasing your work through appropriate platforms for your field

- Building a portfolio of your best work, whether that's writing samples, designing projects, or leadership experiences

→ You are your own best publicist. Promote strategically and authentically.

Remember: When you AMP your digital presence, you're building a professional foundation that will serve you for decades. This isn't about being fake—it's about being strategic with your authenticity.

Platform Strategy: Where to Build Your Professional Presence

Not every platform serves the same purpose in your professional brand. Here's how to think strategically about where to invest your time and energy based on your career goals:

Professional Networking Platforms

LinkedIn (Essential for everyone)

- Your professional headquarters

- Where recruiters and hiring managers look first

- Essential for building industry connections

- Platform for sharing professional insights and achievements

Industry-Specific Portfolio Platforms

Choose based on your field:

Creatives & Designers

- **Behance**: For portfolios in graphic design, photography, fashion, UX/UI, and more.

- **Dribbble**: Focused on short-form, visual design work— great for interface, branding, and product designers.

Coders & Tech Enthusiasts

- **GitHub**: A platform to share coding projects, collaborate with others, and build a reputation in the software development world.

- **Replit**: An interactive coding space for beginners to create and share live code.

Musicians & Audio Creators

- **SoundCloud**: Upload your tracks, grow your fanbase, and connect with fellow musicians and producers.

- **Bandcamp**: Great for selling music and connecting directly with fans.

Video Creators & Filmmakers

- **YouTube**: A widely used platform to share everything from short films to tutorials and vlogs.

- **Vimeo**: A professional video-sharing platform used more by filmmakers, artists, and agencies.

Writers & Bloggers

- **Medium**: A clean, professional platform to publish essays, articles, and thought leadership.

- **Substack**: Ideal for building an email-based newsletter following—great for writers and journalists.

Photographers

- **500px**: A global photography community to share, license, and sell high-quality images.

- **Flickr**: A long-standing platform for both amateur and professional photographers.

Performers & Actors

- **Backstage**: A site for finding casting calls and creating profiles for acting and performance work.

- **Stage32**: A networking platform for film, TV, and theater creatives.

The "Future Boss Test" for Content

Before posting anything anywhere, apply this simple test: "Would I want my future boss, graduate school admissions committee, or dream mentor to see this?"

This doesn't mean everything has to be corporate and boring. It means being intentional about what you share and how you share it.

For example:

- A photo from a weekend hiking trip (shows you're well-rounded and active)

- Sharing an article about industry trends with your thoughtful commentary

- Celebrating a friend's achievement or supporting a cause you believe in

- Photos from parties where alcohol is prominently featured

- Complaints about your current job, school, or boss

- Controversial political statements (unless political advocacy is your career path)

The goal isn't to be perfect or sanitized. It's to be strategic and authentic.

Building Your Professional Content Strategy

Here's where many young professionals get stuck: they understand they should post professional content, but they don't know what that looks like or how often to do it.

Based on my experience mentoring professionals across different industries, here's a content strategy that works:

The 70-20-10 Rule

70% - Industry and Professional Growth Content

- Articles about trends in your field

- Insights from books, courses, or conferences you've attended
- Professional achievements and milestones
- Projects you're working on (with appropriate discretion)

20% - Personal Brand Content

- Your thoughts on industry developments
- Behind-the-scenes looks at your work or studies
- Professional challenges you're navigating and what you're learning

10% - Personal Life Content

- Hobbies and interests that show you're well-rounded
- Travel or cultural experiences
- Causes you support

Content Ideas That Actually Work

Based on what I've seen resonate with hiring managers and industry professionals:

"What I'm Learning" Posts

- Key takeaways from a book in your field
- Insights from a webinar or conference
- Skills you're developing and why they matter

"Behind the Process" Content

- How you approached a challenging project
- Tools and resources you find valuable
- Your problem-solving process

"Industry Insight" Shares

- Commenting thoughtfully on news in your field

- Sharing resources that have helped you grow

- Connecting current events to your area of interest

The Marcus Transformation: A Success Story

Remember Marcus, whose job offer was rescinded? Here's what happened next.

Instead of giving up, Marcus decided to completely rebuild his digital presence using the AMP framework. Here's what he did:

Assess: He discovered that his online presence told the story of someone who wasn't serious about their career. His Instagram was full of party photos, his Twitter had complaints about school and work, and he had no professional presence at all.

Manage: He cleaned up his social media, made his personal accounts private, and removed or retagged inappropriate photos. He also claimed a consistent username across platforms.

Promote: He created a LinkedIn profile showcasing his design work, started a Behance portfolio featuring his best projects, and began sharing thoughtful content about design trends and his creative process.

Six months later, Marcus landed an even better position at a top agency in San Francisco. The creative director who hired him mentioned that Marcus's online portfolio and thoughtful LinkedIn posts were what initially caught their attention.

"Your digital presence told us you were someone who takes their craft seriously," she said. "We could see your growth mindset and your passion for design. That's exactly what we were looking for."

Marcus learned what every successful professional eventually discovers: your online presence isn't separated from your career—it's a fundamental part of it.

Your Digital Brand Action Plan

Here's your roadmap for building a digital presence that opens doors instead of closing them:

Week 1: Assessment

- Complete the Google Test thoroughly
- Audit all your current social media accounts
- Identify what needs to be cleaned up or deleted
- Claim consistent usernames across platforms

Week 2: Management

- Update privacy settings on personal accounts
- Clean up or delete inappropriate content
- Reach out to friends about removing unflattering tags
- Update profile photos to be consistent and professional

Week 3: Foundation Building

- Create or optimize your LinkedIn profile
- Set up your industry-specific portfolio platform
- Write compelling bio descriptions that reflect your goals
- Start following industry leaders and relevant companies

Week 4: Content Strategy

- Plan your content themes using the 70-20-10 rule
- Schedule time for regular posting (aim for 2-3 times per week)
- Start engaging meaningfully with others' content
- Share your first piece of professional content

The Long Game: Building Reputation Over Time

Building a strong digital brand isn't about overnight transformation. It's about consistent, strategic choices that compound over time.

Here's what I tell my mentees: think of your digital presence as a garden. You plant seeds (good content), tend them regularly (consistent posting and engagement), and over time, you harvest the results (opportunities, connections, recognition).

The young professionals who succeed understand that their online presence is working for them 24/7, even when they're not actively job searching. A well-crafted digital brand:

- Attracts opportunities before you even know they exist

- Positions you as a thought leader in your field

- Builds credibility with potential employers, clients, and collaborators

- Creates a network of professional connections

- Documents your growth and achievements over time

Common Mistakes to Avoid

In my years helping young professionals build their digital brands, I've seen the same mistakes repeated over and over. Here are the ones that cost people opportunities:

The "Ghost" Mistake Having no professional online presence at all. In today's world, this makes you look out of touch or like you have something to hide.

The "Overshare" Mistake Posting every personal detail online. Your future boss doesn't need to know about your relationship drama or your opinion on every political issue.

The "Set and Forget" Mistake Creating a LinkedIn profile and never updating it. Your digital presence should evolve as you grow professionally.

The "Inconsistent Brand" Mistake Having completely different personas across platforms. Your professional brand should be consistent, even if different platforms emphasize different aspects of your expertise.

The "Complainer" Mistake Using social media to vent about work, school, or life challenges. This creates a negative first impression that's hard to overcome.

Your Digital Brand Starts Now

Your digital brand isn't something you build someday when you're "ready" to search for a job. It's something you start building today, with every post, every comment, every photo you share.

The difference between young professionals who land great opportunities and those who struggle isn't talent or qualifications—it's often the story their online presence tells about their potential.

In our next chapter, we'll explore how to translate your bold voice and strategic digital presence into ambitious goal setting and career planning. But your digital foundation starts here.

Remember Marcus's story. The opportunities you want are out there, but they might be Googling you before they call. Make sure they like what they find.

What story will your digital presence tell tomorrow? The choice is yours, and the time to start building it is now.

Chapter 3
Building Connections

The presentation was scheduled for 2 PM on a Thursday, and Priya was terrified.

As a junior analyst at our Mumbai office, she'd been asked to present her market research findings to the regional leadership team—including executives from three different countries. Her data was solid, her insights were valuable, but she'd never spoken to such a senior audience before.

"What if I mess up?" she asked me during our prep call the night before. "What if they ask questions I can't answer? What if my English isn't good enough?"

I understood her fear. Priya was brilliant—her analysis had uncovered market opportunities worth millions—but she'd never learned how to translate her expertise into compelling communication. She was about to discover what I've seen proven across five continents: technical competence without communication skills will only get you so far.

The next day, I watched Priya transform before my eyes. She walked into that boardroom, delivered her findings with clarity and confidence, and fielded challenging questions with poise. Not only did the leadership team approve her recommendations— they asked her to lead the implementation across three markets.

After the meeting, the regional VP pulled me aside. "Where did you find her?" he asked. "Her ability to distill complex data into actionable insights and communicate them so clearly—that's exactly the kind of leader we need more of."

Priya learned something that day that changed her entire career trajectory: your ideas are only as powerful as your ability to communicate them.

The Hidden Career Accelerator

Here's what most young professionals don't realize: communication skills aren't a nice-to-have addition to your technical abilities. They're the multiplier that determines how far your expertise will take you.

I've hired and worked with thousands of professionals across different industries and cultures. The ones who advance the fastest aren't always the most technically skilled. They're the ones who can explain complex ideas clearly, present their work compellingly, and build genuine connections with colleagues and clients.

In today's globalized workplace, where you might be collaborating with team members across time zones, presenting to international clients, or networking at industry events, your communication skills literally determine your career ceiling.

But here's the good news: communication excellence isn't a talent you're born with. It's a skill you can develop, practice, and master.

The Three Pillars of Professional Communication

Effective professional communication rests on three foundational pillars:

1. Clarity: Making Complex Ideas Accessible

2. Confidence: Commanding Attention and Respect

3. Connection: Building Relationships That Advance Your Career

Let me show you how to master each one.

Pillar 1: Clarity — Your Ideas Deserve to Be Understood

The most brilliant insight in the world is worthless if no one can understand it. I learned this lesson early in my international career when I watched countless talented professionals struggle to advance simply because they couldn't communicate their value clearly.

The STAR Method for Clear Communication

Whether you're explaining a project update, making a recommendation, or answering interview questions, use this proven framework:

S - Situation: What was the context? **T - Task:** What needed to be accomplished? **A - Action:** What did you do? **R - Result:** What was the outcome?

For example, instead of saying: "I worked on improving our process efficiency and got good results."

Say: "When our team was struggling with delayed project deliveries (Situation), I was asked to identify bottlenecks in our workflow (Task). I analyzed our process, interviewed team members, and implemented a new project tracking system (Action). As a result, we reduced delivery times by 30% and improved client satisfaction scores by 25% (Result)."

See the difference? The second version tells a complete, compelling story that demonstrates your problem-solving abilities and quantifies your impact.

The Power of Strategic Simplicity

Early in my career, I made a classic mistake: I thought using complex language would make me sound more professional. I was wrong. The most effective communicators are those who can take complicated concepts and make them simple without losing their essence.

Here's a framework I teach to all my mentees:

Before communicating anything important, ask yourself:

- What's the core message I need to convey?

- What does my audience need to know to make a decision or take action?

- How can I explain this in the simplest terms possible?

Remember: complexity doesn't demonstrate intelligence. Clarity does.

Pillar 2: Confidence — Your Voice Matters

Confidence in communication isn't about being the loudest person in the room or never feeling nervous. It's about trusting your expertise enough to share it effectively, even when your heart is racing.

Building Unshakeable Communication Confidence

The most effective strategy I've found for building communication confidence is what I call "progressive exposure"— gradually expanding your comfort zone through increasingly challenging speaking opportunities.

Start here:

Level 1: Safe Spaces

- Volunteer to read at religious services

- Lead a workshop for younger students

- Present at local community events

Level 2: Professional Settings

- Volunteer to give updates at team meetings

- Offer to present project findings to your department

- Participate actively in video conference calls

Level 3: High-Stakes Opportunities

- Apply to speak at industry conferences

- Lead client presentations

- Represent your organization at networking events

Each level builds on the last, creating a foundation of positive experiences that fuel your confidence.

Why Your Voice Matters: The Career Impact of Public Speaking

Communication Skills: Effective communication is crucial in almost every job. Public speaking enhances your ability to convey complex ideas clearly, which is essential for leadership roles, presentations, and meetings.

Confidence: Public speaking builds self-confidence. The confidence you build speaking in front of groups transfers directly to job interviews, client presentations, and team meetings.

Leadership: Leaders need to inspire and guide their teams. Public speaking skills help you articulate your vision, motivate colleagues, and drive change.

Persuasion: Whether pitching a project, convincing clients, or negotiating deals, the ability to persuasively present your ideas can significantly impact your career success.

Visibility and Recognition: Being a skilled public speaker can enhance your visibility within your organization and industry, leading to speaking opportunities, board positions, and career advancement.

Overcoming the Fear Factor

Let me share something that might surprise you: even after years of speaking to international audiences, I still get nervous before important presentations. The difference is that I've learned to channel that nervous energy into focused preparation and authentic delivery.

Here's my pre-presentation ritual that works across cultures and contexts:

1. Know Your Material Inside and Out Practice until you can give your presentation without slides. This isn't about memorizing word-for-word—it's about understanding your content so deeply that you can adapt on the fly.

2. Prepare for Questions Anticipate the five most challenging questions you might receive and practice your responses. This preparation gives you confidence to handle unexpected inquiries.

3. Connect with Your audience Early Arrive early and have brief conversations with a few audience members. This transforms a room of strangers into familiar faces.

4. Remember Your Why Before you begin, remind yourself why your message matters. You're not speaking to show off— you're sharing valuable insights that can help others.

Building Your Speaking Skills: A Practical Roadmap

Practice Regularly: The more you practice, the more comfortable you'll become. Record yourself practicing and watch for filler words, unclear pronunciations, and body language habits.

Seek Feedback: Get feedback from colleagues, friends, or mentors to identify areas for improvement.

Join Public Speaking Groups: Organizations like Toastmasters offer a supportive environment for practicing and improving your speaking skills.

Study Great Speakers: Watch speeches by accomplished speakers and analyze their techniques.

Take Public Speaking Courses: Many online and in-person courses are available to help improve public speaking skills.

Start Small: Begin with smaller, less intimidating speaking opportunities and gradually work your way up to larger audiences.

Speaking Organizations and Opportunities

Toastmasters International is a nonprofit organization that helps people improve their public speaking and leadership skills. It offers a structured program where members give speeches, receive constructive feedback, and perform various meeting roles to practice different skills.

However, Toastmasters has an 18-year age requirement. If you're not yet 18 but eager to strengthen your voice, sharpen your communication skills, and practice leadership in a safe, supportive environment, consider joining a **Gavel Club**. These clubs are affiliated with Toastmasters International and follow a similar format, but they're specifically designed for young people. In a Gavel Club, you'll learn how to speak effectively and with purpose, think on your feet, and lead with confidence while receiving helpful feedback from peers. You can even start one at your school or through a community organization. Don't wait until you're 18 to speak up; the world needs your voice now.

Dale Carnegie Training offers public speaking, leadership, and interpersonal skills courses. Their youth programs (ages 14-18) and young professional courses (ages 20-24) are specifically designed to help you excel in interviews, build executive presence, and communicate with impact. These programs are recognized globally and can give you a significant advantage in college applications and early career opportunities.

Other opportunities for improving your public speaking skills include:

The National Speakers Association (NSA) provides resources, networking opportunities, and professional development for aspiring and experienced speakers.

Public Speaking Clubs: Many cities have local public speaking clubs that offer opportunities for practice and feedback.

University Programs: Many universities offer public speaking courses and workshops open to the public.

Online platforms, such as Coursera, Udemy, and LinkedIn Learning, offer courses in public speaking and communication skills.

Enhancing your public speaking abilities can have a profound impact on your career opportunities, as it improves your ability to lead, persuade, and connect with others effectively.

Pillar 3: Connection — Building Professional Relationships

Technical skills might get you in the door, but relationship-building skills determine how far you'll go once you're inside. In my years working across different cultures, I've learned that the ability to build genuine professional connections transcends cultural and linguistic barriers.

The Art of Professional Networking

Networking isn't about collecting business cards or connections on LinkedIn. It's about building mutually beneficial relationships based on genuine interest and shared value.

Here's how to network effectively, whether you're at a conference in Singapore or a local meetup in your hometown:

Before the Event:

- Research who will be attending

- Prepare 2-3 thoughtful questions about industry trends

- Practice your elevator pitch (more on this below)

- Set realistic goals (aim for 3-5 meaningful conversations, not 50 superficial ones)

During the Event:

- Listen more than you talk

- Ask about others' work and challenges before discussing your own

- Look for ways to add value (resources, connections, insights)

- Exchange contact information only when there's genuine mutual interest

After the Event:

- Follow up within 48 hours with a personalized message

- Reference specific points from your conversation

- Offer something valuable (article, introduction, resource)

- Suggest a specific next step if appropriate

Mastering the Elevator Pitch

Your elevator pitch isn't a sales pitch—it's a conversation starter. The goal isn't to tell someone everything about you in 60 seconds. It's to spark their interest enough to want to continue the conversation.

Here's the formula that works across cultures and industries:

"I help [target audience] achieve [specific outcome] by [your unique approach]."

For example: "I help growing tech companies identify and hire top talent by combining data analytics with cultural fit assessment."

Or: "I help small businesses increase their online visibility through strategic social media marketing that actually drives sales."

Practice your elevator pitch until it feels natural, but always be ready to adapt it based on your audience and context.

Learn from the Best: Female Leaders Who Command Attention

Michelle Obama, former First Lady of the United States, is a master of authentic, passionate communication. Her ability to

32

connect with diverse audiences while maintaining authority is something every young woman can learn from. Watch her 2016 "Let Girls Learn" speech—it's a masterclass in speaking directly to your audience's dreams and challenges.

Oprah Winfrey is renowned for her ability to make every person in the audience feel like she's speaking directly to them through her speeches.

Sheryl Sandberg, former COO of Meta and author of "Lean In," is a compelling speaker on leadership. Her TED talks demonstrate how to blend personal stories with professional insights effectively.

Christine Lagarde, President of the European Central Bank and former Managing Director of the International Monetary Fund, demonstrates how to communicate with clarity and authority on complex technical issues.

Indra Nooyi, former CEO of PepsiCo, gives insightful and engaging speeches on leadership. Study how she balances authority with approachability.

Each of these women has mastered the art of commanding attention while remaining authentic. Study their techniques, but remember—your voice and perspective are uniquely yours.

Cross-Cultural Communication: Your Global Advantage

One of the biggest advantages young professionals can develop today is cross-cultural communication competence. In my experience building teams across five continents, the professionals who thrive are those who can adapt their communication style to different cultural contexts while maintaining their authentic voice.

The Strategic Advantage of Multilingual Skills

Learning a new language offers numerous benefits, particularly for someone starting their career:

Enhanced Cognitive Skills - Learning a new language improves memory, problem-solving, and critical thinking. It also enhances multitasking abilities and creativity.

Increased Job Opportunities: Bilingualism opens a broader range of job opportunities in various fields, including international business, diplomacy, tourism, translation, and education.

Competitive Edge: Being bilingual sets you apart from other candidates, making you more attractive to employers, especially in roles that require interaction with international clients or colleagues.

Higher Earning Potential: Many employers are willing to pay a premium for employees who can speak multiple languages. From my experience running international recruitment, I consistently saw bilingual candidates command 8,000 –15,000 higher starting salaries than their monolingual counterparts, depending on the language and market demand.

Cultural Understanding: Learning a new language often involves learning about different cultures, which can enhance interpersonal skills and empathy. This cultural competence is valuable in diverse work environments.

Networking Opportunities: Knowing a second language can expand your professional network, allowing you to connect with colleagues and clients who speak that language, thus opening doors to new business opportunities.

Travel Benefits: Language skills make travel easier and more enjoyable, allowing you to navigate new environments and build connections in different countries.

Personal Growth: Learning a new language can boost self-confidence and provide a sense of accomplishment, contributing to personal growth and development.

Being bilingual is a significant asset for young professionals, demonstrating adaptability, a commitment to personal growth, and the ability to thrive in a globalized workforce. Employers recognize this value—and you should too when negotiating your worth.

Cultural Adaptation Without Losing Authenticity

When I first started working internationally, I made the mistake of trying to completely adapt to each cultural context, essentially becoming a different person in each country. I quickly learned this approach was exhausting and ineffective.

The key is cultural adaptation while maintaining your authentic core. Here's what this looks like in practice:

In High-Context Cultures (Japan, Korea, many Middle Eastern countries):

- Spend more time building relationships before discussing business

- Pay attention to non-verbal cues and what's not being said

- Show respect for hierarchy and formal protocols

- Allow for longer decision-making processes

In Low-Context Cultures (Germany, Netherlands, Scandinavian countries):

- Be direct and explicit in your communication

- Focus on facts, data, and logical arguments

- Respect punctuality and efficiency

- Don't take direct feedback personally

In Relationship-Oriented Cultures (Latin America, Southern Europe, parts of Africa):

- Invest time in personal connections

- Share appropriate personal information

- Be warm and expressive in your communication style

- Understand that business relationships are often personal relationships

The key is adapting your style while maintaining your core message and values.

Your Communication Transformation: A 30-Day Plan

Building professional communication skills takes time, but you can see significant improvement in just 30 days with focused practice:

Week 1: Foundation Building

- Record yourself giving a 2-minute presentation on a topic you know well
- Join a local Toastmasters club or Gavel Club
- Practice the STAR method for describing your experiences
- Start one meaningful professional conversation each day

Week 2: Skill Development

- Practice your elevator pitch with 5 different people
- Attend a networking event or professional meetup
- Volunteer to present something at work or school
- Study one great speaker on YouTube and identify their techniques

Week 3: Real-World Application

- Lead a meeting or group discussion
- Have a difficult conversation you've been avoiding
- Present your ideas to someone in a position of authority
- Ask for feedback on your communication style from a trusted mentor

Week 4: Integration and Growth

- Give a formal presentation to a group of 10 or more people

- Follow up on all the professional connections you've made this month

- Reflect on your progress and identify areas for continued growth

- Set goals for your next 30-day communication challenge

The Compound Effect of Communication Excellence

Here's what I've observed over years of working with young professionals: communication skills compound over time. Every presentation you give builds your confidence. Every meaningful professional relationship you build opens doors to new opportunities. Every difficult conversation you navigate successfully prepares you for bigger challenges.

Priya, the analyst I mentioned at the beginning of this chapter, didn't just succeed in that one presentation. The confidence and skills she developed led to more speaking opportunities, which led to greater visibility, which led to leadership roles she never could have imagined when she was terrified of presenting to a small group.

Today, she's the VP of Strategy for the entire Asia-Pacific region, regularly presenting to boards of directors and representing the company at international conferences. All because she learned to communicate her expertise with clarity, confidence, and connection.

Your Voice Is Your Superpower

Your technical skills, your creativity, your problem-solving ability—all of these matter. But your communication skills are what will amplify everything else you bring to the table.

In a world where remote work is increasingly common, where teams are globally distributed, and where change happens at the speed of technology, the ability to communicate clearly and build genuine connections isn't just a career advantage—it's a career necessity.

The good news? You don't have to be a natural extrovert or born speaker to excel at professional communication. You just need to be willing to practice, learn, and gradually expand your comfort zone.

Your ideas deserve to be heard. Your insights deserve to influence decisions. Your voice deserves to be part of important conversations.

The only question is: are you ready to develop the communication skills that will make it happen?

In our next chapter, we'll explore how to channel your bold voice, strategic digital presence, and compelling communication skills into setting and achieving ambitious goals. But everything we build going forward rests on this foundation: your ability to share your ideas with clarity, confidence, and connection.

Your voice is your superpower. It's time to learn how to use it.

Chapter 4
Be Ambitious

The text message came at 11:47 PM on a Sunday, and it made me smile wider than any promotion announcement ever had.

"Erica, I got it! The NASA internship—they said yes!" It was from Zara, a brilliant 19-year-old engineering student I'd been mentoring for the past year. "Six months ago, I was too scared to even apply. Thank you for teaching me it's okay to want impossible things."

Six months earlier, Zara had approached me after a talk I gave at her university in Toronto. She was majoring in aerospace engineering but was convinced she wasn't "good enough" for competitive opportunities. "I don't want to seem too ambitious," she'd said. "People might think I'm being unrealistic."

That conversation broke my heart—and fired me up. Here was a young woman with exceptional talent, stellar grades, and innovative project ideas, apologizing for wanting to reach for the stars. Literally.

I told her something that I wish every young woman understood: ambition isn't arrogance. It's not greed. It's not "too much." Ambition is simply the courage to match your goals to your potential instead of shrinking them to fit other people's expectations.

Today, Zara is working on projects that could revolutionize space exploration. Her ambition didn't just change her trajectory—it put her on a path to change the world.

The Permission You Don't Need to Ask For

Here's what I've learned from mentoring ambitious young women across five continents: the biggest barrier to achievement isn't lack of talent, opportunity, or even resources. It's the internalized belief that wanting more is somehow wrong.

We've been conditioned to believe that ambition in women is unattractive, aggressive, or selfish. That good girls should be grateful for what they have and shouldn't reach for more. That asking for the promotion, applying for the stretch opportunity, or starting the business is "too much."

I'm here to tell you that's complete nonsense.

Ambition is the strong desire to achieve something meaningful, typically requiring determination and hard work. It involves setting high goals for yourself and striving to reach them. Ambition drives you to pursue your passions, excel in your career, and make a significant impact on the world.

More importantly: it's okay to want more responsibility, more recognition, and more success. Never let anyone make you feel guilty for your ambitions.

Before we dive into how to channel your ambition effectively, I want you to think about your own relationship with wanting more:

- What dream have you kept small because someone called it "unrealistic"?

- What opportunity haven't you pursued because you worried about seeming "too ambitious"?

- Who in your life models healthy ambition? What can you learn from them?

- If you knew you couldn't fail, what would you try tomorrow?

Now, let's talk about how to transform that ambition into achievement.

The Architecture of Ambitious Achievement

Ambition without strategy is just dreaming. Ambition without action is just wishful thinking. But ambition combined with strategic planning and persistent execution? That's how you change your life—and potentially the world.

Here's how to build your ambition into sustainable success:

1. Define Success on Your Own Terms

Before anyone else tells you what you should want, get crystal clear on what success actually means to you. Not your parents' definition. Not society's definition. Yours.

I've mentored young women who thought they wanted to be doctors until they realized they were more interested in healthcare policy. Others who thought they wanted to start businesses until they discovered they preferred being the strategic advisor helping others build companies.

Here's a framework that works:

Short-term goals (1-2 years): What skills, experiences, or achievements will position you for bigger opportunities?

Medium-term goals (3-5 years): What role, impact, or recognition do you want to achieve?

Long-term vision (10+ years): What legacy do you want to build? What change do you want to create?

For example, if you're passionate about environmental sustainability:

- Short-term: Complete coursework in environmental science, intern at a renewable energy company

- Medium-term: Lead sustainability initiatives at a major corporation or start an environmental consulting firm

- Long-term: Influence policy that creates meaningful environmental change

2. Invest Strategically in Your Development

Ambition requires continuous learning, but not all education is created equal. Be strategic about where you invest your time and energy.

Here's something crucial: don't limit your educational choices based on what's traditionally "acceptable" for women. If you're brilliant at mathematics, don't default to teaching just because it's expected. If you love building things, don't avoid engineering because you'll be one of the few women in the program.

Absolutely pursue nursing, fashion, education, or any field that genuinely excites you—and pursue it with excellence. But don't choose these fields simply because they're "appropriate" for women. And definitely don't avoid other fields because they're not.

Some of the most exciting, impactful, and well-paying careers today are in fields where women are still underrepresented—and that represents opportunity. If you're curious, analytical, or love solving complex problems, strongly consider STEM: Science, Technology, Engineering, and Mathematics.

STEM careers aren't just about high salaries (though they often are well-paid). They're about having the technical skills to solve humanity's biggest challenges—from climate change to disease to space exploration. These fields give you the power to innovate, influence, and lead in the industries that are literally shaping our future.

Women belong in every boardroom, laboratory, startup, and coding bootcamp. When you choose a bold educational path, you're not just building your own career—you're opening doors for every girl who comes after you.

Don't wait to be invited into the room. Walk in, sit down, and make your expertise known.

Real Women Breaking Ground in STEM

Tu Youyou (China): A pharmaceutical chemist who became the first Chinese woman to win a Nobel Prize. She discovered artemisinin, a breakthrough malaria treatment that has saved millions of lives worldwide.

Dr. Katie Bouman (USA): She helped develop the algorithm that produced the first-ever image of a black hole, making the invisible visible and advancing our understanding of the universe.

Gitanjali Rao (India/USA): Named Time Magazine's "Kid of the Year" for her work using technology to tackle global problems like contaminated water detection and cyberbullying prevention—proving that ambition has no age limit.

Dr. Fei-Fei Li (China/USA): An artificial intelligence pioneer who led AI development at Google and now teaches at Stanford while advocating for ethical technology development that serves all of humanity.

These women didn't wait for permission—they followed their curiosity, trusted their abilities, and changed the world.

Careers Where You Can Be the First—or the Best!

The opportunities in emerging fields are limitless:

- **Software Engineer** (building the applications that will run our future)

- **Aerospace Scientist** (designing the technology that will take us to Mars)

- **Environmental Engineer** (creating solutions for climate change)

- **Data Scientist** (finding patterns that reveal new insights)

- **Biomedical Researcher** (developing treatments that will save lives)

- **Cybersecurity Specialist** (protecting our digital world)

- **Robotics Designer** (creating technology that enhances human capability)

- **Climate Scientist** (understanding and addressing our planet's biggest challenge)

- **AI Ethics Consultant** (ensuring technology serves humanity responsibly)

- **Space Mission Analyst** (planning humanity's expansion beyond Earth)

Take a moment right now: write down one subject that genuinely excites you. Now research three careers that use that skill at the highest level. What would it take to get there? What's stopping you from pursuing that path?

3. Seek Challenges That Stretch Your Capabilities

Ambitious people don't choose the easy path—they choose the growth path. This means actively seeking opportunities that feel just beyond your current comfort zone.

In my experience mentoring high achievers, the ones who advance fastest are those who consistently choose the challenging assignment over the easy one, the stretch role over the safe one, the ambitious project over the guaranteed success.

Here's how to apply this practically:

- When given project options, choose the one that will teach you the most, not the one you're already good at

- Volunteer for assignments that require you to develop new skills

- Apply for opportunities even when you don't meet every qualification (studies show women apply only when they meet 100% of requirements, while men apply at 60%)

4. Build Systems That Support Your Ambitions

Ambition without discipline is just enthusiasm. The most successful people I know aren't just passionate—they're systematic about pursuing their goals.

Create daily routines that prioritize your ambitions:

- Dedicate specific time blocks to skill development

- Set weekly goals that connect to your larger objectives

- Track your progress consistently

- Eliminate activities that don't serve your goals

For example, if your ambition is to start a sustainable fashion company, your daily routine might include: morning time for industry research, lunch breaks for sketching designs, evenings for building your business knowledge through courses or reading.

5. Find Guides Who've Walked Your Path

Every ambitious person needs guides—people who have achieved what you're working toward and can help you navigate the journey more effectively.

But here's what most people get wrong about mentorship: they expect one person to provide all the guidance they need. Instead, build a diverse advisory network:

- **Industry mentor**: Someone successful in your chosen field

- **Skills mentor**: Someone who excels at specific capabilities you need to develop

- **Leadership mentor**: Someone who can guide your overall professional development

- **Life mentor**: Someone who helps you balance ambition with well-being

Don't just ask "Will you be my mentor?" Instead, seek specific guidance: "I'm working on developing my public speaking skills. Could I get your advice on my next presentation?"

6. Curate Your Circle Strategically

Show me your friends, and I'll show you your future. The people you spend time with significantly influence your level of ambition and achievement.

Actively seek out relationships with people who:

- Challenge you to think bigger
- Support your goals even when others don't understand them
- Share valuable resources and opportunities
- Hold you accountable to your commitments
- Model the kind of success you want to achieve

This might mean joining professional organizations, attending industry events, or participating in online communities related to your field of interest.

7. Create Opportunities Instead of Waiting for Them

Ambitious people understand a fundamental truth: the best opportunities aren't posted on job boards. They're created by people who see problems and propose solutions.

In every organization, there are inefficiencies, unmet needs, and improvement opportunities. Instead of waiting for someone else to address them, be the person who says: "I see this challenge, I have ideas for solving it, and I'd like to lead the solution."

This approach works whether you're in school, at an internship, or in your first job. Initiative-takers get noticed, get opportunities, and get promoted.

8. Reframe Setbacks as Intelligence Gathering

Here's something nobody tells you about ambition: the bigger your goals, the more rejection you'll face. This isn't a bug in the system—it's a feature. Rejection is how you learn what you need to improve.

When you don't get the internship, the admission, or the opportunity you wanted, don't just feel disappointed. Get curious:

- What specific skills or experiences were they looking for that you didn't have?

- How can you develop those capabilities?

- What can you do differently in your next application?

- Who could provide guidance on strengthening your candidacy?

Then create a plan to address those gaps and try again. Resilience isn't about bouncing back—it's about bouncing forward with new knowledge and capabilities.

9. Maintain Insatiable Curiosity

Ambitious people are learning machines. They understand that in a rapidly changing world, curiosity isn't just helpful—it's essential for staying relevant and competitive.

Make continuous learning a non-negotiable part of your routine:

- Read industry publications and thought leadership content

- Attend workshops, conferences, and webinars

- Take online courses that build relevant skills

- Seek diverse perspectives and challenge your assumptions

- Ask better questions instead of just seeking validation for your existing ideas

10. Embrace the Growth Mindset

Your current abilities are not your permanent limitations. With effort, strategy, and persistence, you can develop almost any skill you need to achieve your ambitions.

This mindset shift is crucial because it changes how you approach challenges:

- Instead of "I'm not good at public speaking," think "I haven't developed strong public speaking skills yet"

- Instead of "I'm not a math person," think "I need to find better strategies for learning mathematical concepts"

- Instead of "I could never start a business," think "I need to learn more about entrepreneurship and business development"

The word "yet" is transformative. It acknowledges where you are while affirming where you can go.

Learning from Ambitious Trailblazers

Let me share stories of two women whose ambition literally changed the world—not because they were born extraordinary, but because they refused to accept limitations others tried to place on them.

Marie Curie: Ambition Fueled by Discovery and Determination

Marie Curie wasn't just brilliant—she was strategically ambitious in a world that systematically excluded women from science. Born in Poland in 1867, she moved to Paris to pursue education that was forbidden to women in her home country.

Think about the level of ambition this required: leaving everything familiar, living in poverty while studying physics and mathematics, persisting despite professors and peers who believed women couldn't understand science. She didn't just want to learn—she wanted to discover. She didn't just want to participate—she wanted to lead.

Her ambition paid off in ways that changed human history. She became the first woman to win a Nobel Prize, then the first person ever to win Nobel Prizes in two different sciences (Physics and Chemistry). She discovered radium and polonium, coined the term "radioactivity," and laid the groundwork for cancer treatments still saving lives today.

What I find most inspiring about Marie's story isn't just what she achieved—it's how she defined ambition. For her, ambition wasn't about fame or recognition. It was about pushing the boundaries of human knowledge, even when that work put her health at risk.

As she said: "One never notices what has been done; one can only see what remains to be done."

That's the mindset of sustainable ambition—always focused on the next challenge, the next discovery, the next way to contribute.

Malala Yousafzai: Ambition in the Face of Danger

Malala's story shows us that ambition doesn't require adult credentials or perfect circumstances. Her ambition began with a notebook and the belief that every girl deserved education.

At 11 years old—younger than many reading this book—she began blogging anonymously for the BBC about life under Taliban rule and threats to girls' education. Think about the courage this required: speaking truth to power when that power had already demonstrated its willingness to use violence.

As her voice grew louder, so did the danger. In 2012, the Taliban tried to silence her with an assassination attempt. Instead of retreating, she returned stronger. She became a global advocate for education, the youngest Nobel Peace Prize laureate at 17, and a living example of how ambition combined with moral courage can change the world.

What strikes me about Malala's ambition is how it's rooted in service to others. She didn't want fame—she wanted justice. She didn't seek attention—she sought change. Her ambition was never about personal advancement but about creating a world where every girl could pursue her own ambitions through education.

As she says: "I tell my story not because it is unique, but because it is the story of many girls."

That's ambition at its finest—using your platform to amplify others, not just yourself.

Practical Ambition: Your Action Blueprint

Now that you understand what healthy ambition looks like, here's how to channel it into concrete action:

Daily Ambition Practices

Visualize with Specificity: Don't just imagine "being successful." Visualize exactly what your ideal day looks like 5 years from now. Where are you working? What problems are you solving? Who are you collaborating with? What impact are you making?

Commit to Continuous Growth: Dedicate at least 30 minutes daily to learning something that advances your goals. This could be reading industry publications, taking online courses, practicing new skills, or studying successful people in your field.

Acknowledge Progress: Document and celebrate your wins, no matter how small. Keep a "success journal" where you record daily achievements, lessons learned, and progress made toward your goals.

Maintain Optimistic Persistence: Challenges are inevitable, but your response to them determines your trajectory. When you face setbacks, ask "What can I learn from this?" and "How can this redirect me toward something better?"

Seek Strategic Feedback: Regularly ask mentors, peers, and supervisors for specific feedback on your progress. Don't just ask "How am I doing?" Ask "What's one skill I should develop to reach the next level?" or "What would make my work more impactful?"

Ambitious Action Steps You Can Take This Month

Start Something New: Identify a need in your school or community and create a solution. This could be starting a club, organizing an event, or launching an initiative that addresses a problem you care about.

Build Something That Showcases Your Capabilities: Whether it's developing an app, creating content, conducting research, or designing a product, having tangible work to show demonstrates your abilities more powerfully than any resume.

Compete to Grow: Enter competitions in your areas of interest. The goal isn't just winning—it's pushing yourself to perform at higher levels and gaining experience with high-stakes performance.

Gain Real-World Experience: Seek internships, volunteer opportunities, or part-time work in your field of interest. Experience beats classroom learning when it comes to understanding what you actually want to do with your life.

Share Your Voice: Create content that showcases your expertise and interests. This builds your personal brand while forcing you to articulate your ideas clearly and consistently.

Develop Strategic Skills: Choose new skills based on what will advance your specific goals, not just what seems interesting. If you want to work internationally, learn languages. If you want to start a business, learn financial modeling.

Practice High-Stakes Communication: Join speaking organizations, volunteer to present at events, or create video content. Your ability to communicate your ideas will significantly impact your ability to advance your ambitions.

Become an Expert in Your Field: Read industry publications, follow thought leaders, and stay current with trends and developments. Knowledge is only powerful when it's current and comprehensive.

Invest in Formal Learning: Take courses that provide structured learning and credentials. Focus on skills that are directly applicable to your career goals.

Use Your Voice for Change: If you see problems in your community or industry, don't just complain—act. Advocacy work develops leadership skills while contributing to causes you care about.

From New Girl to Student Body President: My Ambition Story

Let me share the moment that taught me what real ambition looks like.

I was 17, living in Peoria, Illinois, surrounded by close friends and the comfortable familiarity of a place I'd called home for years. Then my father, who worked for Caterpillar, received a transfer to England. Suddenly, I was packing my life into suitcases and preparing to finish high school at the American Community School in London—a place where I knew absolutely no one.

Walking into that co-ed international school after years in an all-girls environment felt overwhelming. The easy choice would have been to keep my head down, focus on academics, and just get through the year. But something inside me whispered: "Be ambitious."

During my first week, I saw posters around school announcing student body president elections. I had no friends to campaign for me, no reputation to build on, no connections to leverage. What I had was something my father had instilled in me since childhood: the belief that I could accomplish anything I set my mind to.

So I decided to run.

I started by doing something that would become central to my leadership philosophy: I listened. I spent the next week asking students what mattered most to them, what changes they wanted to see, what problems needed solving. I wasn't trying to impose my agenda—I was trying to understand theirs.

When election day came, I stood on that stage, my voice trembling and my knees shaking, but with purpose in my heart. I delivered a speech that reflected what I'd learned from my fellow students, speaking to their concerns and their hopes.

To my amazement, I won.

That experience taught me something I've carried through every stage of my career: ambition isn't about already having the spotlight. It's about having the courage to step into it, even when no one knows your name. It's about believing in your ability to add value, even when you can't yet prove it.

More importantly, it taught me that authentic ambition starts with service—understanding what others need and positioning yourself to help provide it.

The Ripple Effects of Strategic Ambition

Here's what I've observed from years of mentoring ambitious young women: the ones who achieve the most aren't those with the biggest dreams—they're those who combine big dreams with strategic action and genuine service to others.

Zara's NASA internship didn't just change her trajectory. It positioned her to work on projects that could advance space exploration for all humanity. My student body presidency didn't just build my confidence—it taught me leadership skills I've used to build teams across five continents.

When your ambition serves something larger than yourself, it becomes sustainable and fulfilling in ways that purely personal ambition never can.

Your Ambitious Future Starts Now

Ambition is about striving for excellence and not settling for mediocrity. By being ambitious, you set yourself on a path to achieving your dreams and making a significant impact on the world.

But here's what I want you to understand: your ambition doesn't need anyone else's permission or approval. You don't need to wait until you're older, more experienced, or more qualified.

You can start being ambitious today. In fact, you should start today.

The world needs what you have to offer. It needs your fresh perspective, your energy, your creativity, and your solutions to problems that previous generations haven't been able to solve.

Your ambition isn't selfish—it's necessary. When you pursue your goals with determination and integrity, you create opportunities not just for yourself but for everyone who comes after you.

So dream bigger. Then work smarter. Build systems that support your goals. Surround yourself with people who believe in your potential. Learn continuously. Take strategic risks. Serve others through your achievements.

Most importantly: never apologize for wanting more. The world is waiting for you to claim your place in it.

In our next chapter, we'll explore the final element of the BAD framework: how to be determined in the face of obstacles, setbacks, and people who tell you your ambitions are too big. Because ambition without determination is just wishful thinking—but ambition plus determination? That's how you change the world.

Your ambitious journey starts now. What impossible thing will you make possible?

Chapter 5
Be Determined

The phone rang at 3:17 AM, and I knew it was going to be one of those calls that changes everything.

"Erica," came Alessia's voice through my phone, shaky but determined. "I didn't get the medical school acceptance. The rejection letter came today."

I had been mentoring Alessia for two years, watching her navigate the grueling path toward becoming a doctor. She'd spent countless hours studying for the MCAT, volunteering at hospitals, conducting research, and maintaining a near-perfect GPA. This was her second rejection cycle, and I could hear the exhaustion in her voice.

"I keep thinking maybe I should just give up," she continued. "Maybe I'm not meant for this. Maybe I should find something easier."

I understood her pain. Rejection at this level—after investing years of your life toward a dream—feels like the universe telling you to quit. But I also knew something about Alessia that she was struggling to remember in that moment: she was built for exactly this kind of challenge.

"Alessia," I said, "can I tell you what I see when I look at your journey so far?"

What I saw was a young woman who had already demonstrated extraordinary determination. She'd overcome a learning disability that made standardized tests challenging. She'd worked two part-time jobs to pay for her MCAT prep courses. She'd maintained her grades while caring for her sick grandmother. She hadn't failed at becoming a doctor—she was still in the process of becoming one.

Today, Dr. Alessia Rodriguez is completing her residency in pediatric oncology, working with children who face their own battles with determination every day. Her rejection wasn't the end of her story—it was the chapter that taught her that determination isn't about never facing obstacles. It's about never letting obstacles have the final word.

The Myth of Linear Success

Here's what Instagram doesn't show you: every successful person you admire has a graveyard of failures behind them. The entrepreneur whose company is now worth millions? She failed at her first three startups. The Olympic athlete whose gold medal ceremony brought you to tears? She didn't make her high school varsity team.

We live in a culture that celebrates outcomes but ignores process. We see the Nobel Prize winner but not the decades of experiments that didn't work. We see the bestselling author but not the manuscript rejections. We see the Fortune 500 CEO but not the promotions she didn't get.

This cultural blindness to struggle creates a dangerous myth: that success should be easy, and if it's not, you're probably not meant for it.

I'm here to tell you that's complete nonsense.

Determination is the firmness of purpose—the resolve to achieve your goals despite challenges and setbacks. It involves persistence, resilience, and a never-give-up attitude. More importantly, it's the understanding that obstacles aren't evidence that you're on the wrong path. They're evidence that you're on a path worth traveling.

Before we dive into how to build unshakeable determination, I want you to think about your own relationship with obstacles:

- When you face a setback, what story do you tell yourself? Does that story serve your goals?

56

- Think of someone you admire. What challenges do you think they overcame that you don't see?

- What would you attempt if you knew that failure was just information, not judgment?

Now, let's talk about how to build the kind of determination that turns obstacles into stepping stones.

The Architecture of Unshakeable Determination

Determination isn't a personality trait you're born with or without. It's a skill you can develop through specific practices and mindset shifts. Here's how to build determination that will serve you throughout your life:

1. Create a Goal Architecture That Sustains Motivation

Vague goals create weak determination. "I want to be successful" won't sustain you through difficult moments. "I want to develop clean water solutions for underserved communities by age 30" will.

Here's how to structure goals that build determination:

Ultimate Vision (10+ years): What impact do you want to have on the world? **Strategic Milestones (3-5 years):** What capabilities, positions, or achievements will position you to create that impact? **Tactical Goals (1-2 years):** What specific skills, experiences, or credentials do you need to develop? **Monthly Targets:** What actions will you take this month to move toward your tactical goals? **Weekly Actions:** What will you do this week to hit your monthly targets?

For example, if your ultimate vision is to become a project manager who helps organizations implement sustainable practices:

- Strategic milestone: Get hired as a junior project manager at a company focused on sustainability

- Tactical goal: Earn project management certification and gain experience leading environmental initiatives

- Monthly target: Complete one section of your certification and volunteer to lead a sustainability project at school

- Weekly action: Study for 5 hours and attend one environmental organization meeting

This architecture ensures that even when you face setbacks at one level, you maintain forward momentum at others.

2. Build Systems That Support Persistence

Determination isn't about willpower—it's about designing your life to make persistence easier than quitting.

Create systems that build momentum:

Time Architecture: Block specific times for working toward your goals. Treat these appointments with yourself as seriously as you would a job interview.

Environment Design: Set up your physical space to support your goals. If you're learning to code, have your laptop ready with bookmarks to coding tutorials. If you're training for athletics, lay out your workout clothes the night before.

Accountability Structures: Share your goals with people who will check on your progress. This could be a mentor, study group, or even social media accountability.

Progress Tracking: Keep visible records of your advancement. This could be a checklist, progress photos, skill assessments, or a success journal.

3. Reframe Challenges as Intelligence Gathering

Every challenge you face is giving you data about what you need to develop, where you need to grow, and how you can improve your approach. The key is learning to see obstacles as information rather than indictment.

When you encounter a difficult situation:

Ask intelligence-gathering questions:

- What is this challenge teaching me about what I need to learn?

- How can I approach this differently?

- Who has solved similar problems, and what can I learn from their approach?

- What support or resources do I need to tackle this effectively?

Seek strategic help: Getting support isn't admitting weakness—it's demonstrating wisdom. When you're assigned a challenging project, actively seek guidance from mentors, teachers, or colleagues who have relevant experience.

Document lessons learned: Keep a record of what you discover through each challenge. This builds your confidence by showing you how much you're growing, and it creates a playbook for handling future obstacles.

4. Transform Failures into Fuel

Here's what I've learned from mentoring high achievers across different industries: the people who succeed aren't those who never fail. They're those who fail faster, learn quicker, and iterate better.

When you don't get the audition, election, internship, or opportunity you wanted:

Get specific feedback: Don't just accept "we went with someone else." Ask: "What specific skills or experiences would have made me a stronger candidate?" "What can I do to improve for next time?"

Conduct your own analysis: What went well? What could you have done differently? What assumptions did you make that proved incorrect?

Create an improvement plan: Based on the feedback and your analysis, what specific actions will you take to strengthen your candidacy for similar opportunities?

Set a timeline for trying again: Don't let rejection become permanent. Decide when you'll apply for similar opportunities again, and use the interim time to address the gaps you identified.

Remember: rejection is often about fit, timing, or competition—not about your fundamental worth or potential.

5. Protect Your Mental Energy Like Your Most Valuable Resource

Determination requires sustained mental energy, and our modern world is designed to scatter your attention. Protecting your focus isn't just about productivity—it's about preserving the mental clarity needed to persist through challenges.

Design your environment for focus:

- Use apps or settings that limit social media during work/study times

- Create physical spaces dedicated to important work

- Establish boundaries around your goal-pursuit time

Practice energy management:

- Identify when you have the most mental energy and use those times for your most important work

- Build rest and recovery into your schedule— determination requires sustainability

- Say no to commitments that don't serve your primary goals

6. Understand the Compound Nature of Progress

Most meaningful goals don't show linear progress. You study for weeks before suddenly understanding a complex concept. You practice for months before having a breakthrough performance. You build for years before achieving overnight success.

The key to persistence is understanding that invisible progress is still progress:

Trust the process during plateau periods: Just because you can't see dramatic changes doesn't mean nothing is happening. Skills, strength, and understanding often develop beneath the surface before becoming visible.

Measure inputs, not just outputs: Track your effort and consistency, not just results. If you're studying for 10 hours a week consistently, that's success regardless of your current test scores.

Celebrate small wins: Acknowledge improvement, no matter how minor. Did you study for longer today? Understand a concept that confused you yesterday? Complete a challenging workout? These are victories worth recognizing.

7. Create Feedback Loops That Accelerate Growth

Determined people don't just seek feedback—they create systems for getting better information more frequently.

Ask specific questions: Instead of "How did I do?" ask "What's one thing I could do differently next time to improve the outcome?" Instead of "Any feedback?" ask "What skill should I focus on developing to reach the next level?"

Seek diverse perspectives: Get feedback from multiple sources—peers, mentors, supervisors, and even people who might disagree with your approach.

Implement rapidly: Don't just collect feedback—act on it quickly. The faster you can implement suggestions and see results, the more motivated you'll be to continue seeking improvement.

8. Curate a Circle That Fuels Persistence

Determination is partly an individual trait, but it's significantly influenced by the people around you. Surround yourself strategically with people who support your long-term vision, even when short-term results are discouraging.

Seek out:

- People who have achieved what you're working toward

- Peers who are on similar journeys and can relate to your challenges

- Mentors who can provide perspective during difficult moments

- Cheerleaders who believe in your potential even when you doubt yourself

Limit time with:

- People who consistently discourage your goals

- Those who try to convince you to "be realistic" (often code for "give up")

- Individuals who celebrate your failures more than your successes

Join communities: Look for groups, organizations, or online communities related to your goals where persistence and growth are celebrated.

Why Determination Matters More Than Ever

In today's rapidly changing world, determination isn't just helpful—it's essential. Here's why:

Career Development: The average person changes careers multiple times. Determination helps you navigate transitions, acquire new skills, and persist through the learning curves that come with change.

Professional Recognition: Employers don't just hire skills—they hire character. Determination signals that you'll persist through difficult projects, learn from setbacks, and continue growing even when things get challenging.

Leadership Opportunities: Leaders are people who continue moving forward when others give up. Your determination becomes a beacon for others and positions you for increasing responsibility.

The Determination Gap: Why This Matters Especially for Young Women

Here's a reality we need to acknowledge: from early childhood, girls are often socialized to be "good" and "nice"—qualities that can sometimes be interpreted as being compliant rather than determined. We're taught to avoid conflict, not make waves, and accept "no" gracefully.

These social expectations can undermine determination in subtle but significant ways:

We're taught to avoid appearing "pushy" or "aggressive." We're encouraged to accept rejection politely rather than seek feedback. We're praised for being "easy to work with" rather than persistent. We're told that wanting too much makes us unlikeable.

The statistics bear this out: men typically apply for jobs when they meet about 60% of the qualifications, while women apply only when they meet 100% of them.

What this means for you: many brilliant young women are self-selecting out of opportunities they could absolutely handle. They're waiting until they feel 100% ready, which often means missing chances for growth and development.

Your takeaway: don't underestimate your abilities or overestimate what's required. If an opportunity excites you and aligns with your goals, apply anyway. Embracing challenges before you feel fully prepared often leads to the fastest growth.

Determination isn't about being aggressive or unlikeable. It's about having enough respect for your goals to persist in pursuing them, even when the path gets difficult.

Learning from Determined Trailblazers

J.K. Rowling: Before Harry Potter became a global phenomenon, Rowling faced twelve publisher rejections. Twelve. She was a single mother, living on welfare, writing in cafes because she couldn't afford to heat her apartment. Her determination wasn't just about wanting to be published—it was about believing in her story enough to keep trying when everyone else said no.

Simone Biles: Beyond her incredible athletic achievements, Simone has shown determination in advocating for athlete mental health and speaking out about abuse in her sport. Her decision to prioritize her well-being during the Tokyo Olympics, despite enormous pressure, showed a different kind of determination—the courage to make difficult decisions that serve her long-term goals rather than short-term expectations.

Serena Williams: Throughout her career, Serena faced not just athletic challenges but also racism, sexism, and criticism about her appearance and behavior. Her determination wasn't just about winning matches—it was about changing the conversation around what female athletes could be and how they could show up in their sport.

Jackie Joyner-Kersee: Competing with severe asthma, Jackie became one of the greatest all-around athletes in history. She won multiple Olympic golds in heptathlon and long jump, proving that physical limitations don't have to limit achievements when combined with extraordinary determination.

Katie Ledecky: Her dominance in distance swimming didn't happen overnight. Katie's determination shows up in her training—she's known for her incredible work ethic and ability to maintain intensity through grueling practice sessions year after year.

Mia Hamm: A pioneer in women's soccer, Mia's determination helped build not just her own career but an entire sport. She played through injuries, fought for equal pay and recognition, and helped establish women's soccer as a viable professional sport in America.

What these women have in common isn't that they never faced obstacles—it's that they never let obstacles have the final word.

Practical Determination: Your Daily Toolkit

The Daily Practices That Build Determination

Self-discipline isn't about depriving yourself—it's about making choices that serve your long-term goals even when they conflict with short-term desires.

Build determination through:

- Consistent daily actions that move you toward your goals

- Keeping commitments you make to yourself

- Choosing growth over comfort in small decisions

- Maintaining routines that support your objectives

Conquering Procrastination: The Dream Delayer

Let's address the elephant in the room: procrastination isn't really about poor time management. It's usually about fear, perfectionism, or self-doubt masquerading as "I'll do it later."

Procrastination whispers convincing lies:

- "You're not ready yet"

- "Let's wait until you have more time"

- "It needs to be perfect before you start"

- "What if you fail?"

The truth is: the perfect moment rarely comes, and waiting too long steals opportunities. Young women are often raised to be careful, to get things "just right." But this can turn healthy preparation into paralyzing perfectionism.

Why does this matter? Because your dreams can't afford to live in "someday." The internship application, the creative project, the leadership opportunity, the business idea in your notes app—they all need you to act now.

Remember: imperfect action beats perfect inaction every time.

Ask yourself:

- What have you been putting off that would move you closer to your goals?

- Are you avoiding this because you fear failure, or because you fear success?

- What would change in your life if you took action on this today?

Develop a Growth-Oriented Mindset

Determination isn't about being relentlessly positive—it's about maintaining a growth-oriented perspective that sees challenges as development opportunities rather than threats.

Reframe your internal dialogue:

- Instead of "I failed," think "I learned what doesn't work"

- Instead of "I'm not good at this," think "I'm not good at this yet"

- Instead of "This is too hard," think "This will help me grow"

- Instead of "I should give up," think "I should try a different approach"

Harness the Power of Visualization

Your brain doesn't distinguish between vividly imagined experiences and real ones. Regular visualization literally rewires your neural pathways to support success.

Make visualization specific and sensory:

- What exactly will achieving your goal look like?

- How will it feel in your body?

- What will you hear, see, and experience?

- Who will be there to celebrate with you?

One powerful tool for this is creating a vision board.

A vision board isn't just a craft project—it's a daily reminder of who you're becoming and what you're working toward.

Your vision board should include:

- Images that represent your goals and dreams

- Quotes that inspire and motivate you

- Colors and designs that energize you

- Specific achievements you want to accomplish

How to Create One:

- Use a poster board or digital tools like Canva or Pinterest

- Gather images, quotes, and words that represent your goals

- Choose visuals that create an emotional response

- Arrange them in a way that feels inspiring to you

- Place it where you'll see it daily—bedroom wall, bathroom mirror, phone wallpaper

Why it works: Your brain focuses on what it sees repeatedly. Daily visualization trains your mind to recognize opportunities and stay motivated toward your goals.

The Power of Physical and Mental Resilience

Build Physical Stamina That Supports Mental Determination

Physical and mental resilience are interconnected. Regular exercise doesn't just improve your physical health—it builds your capacity to persist through mental and emotional challenges.

Benefits for determination:

- Exercise releases endorphins that improve mood and motivation
- Physical challenges build confidence in your ability to push through discomfort
- Regular activity improves sleep and energy levels needed for persistent effort
- Working out provides a healthy outlet for frustration and stress

Create Momentum Through Recognition

Determination requires sustainable motivation, and sustainable motivation requires regular recognition of progress.

Build a celebration system:

- Acknowledge daily efforts, not just outcomes
- Share wins with your support system
- Reward yourself for hitting milestones
- Keep a success journal to track progress over time
- Celebrate learning and growth, even when results aren't perfect

A Story of Unstoppable Determination

Brooke: The Girl Who Refused to Give Up

Brooke had always dreamed of becoming a nurse. She wanted to hold someone's hand during a scary diagnosis, helping people feel safe and cared for. But there was one class standing in her way: Pathophysiology—a big, intimidating word for a class that teaches what happens to the body when it gets sick. And it was really hard.

Brooke tried everything. She made colorful flashcards, joined study groups, took practice quizzes, and stayed up late reviewing every chapter. She gave it everything she had. However, when the final grades were announced, she had failed. It was heartbreaking.

But she didn't give up.

She signed up again the next semester, more determined than ever. But life threw her another curveball, and despite her efforts, she failed *again*. Now she was down to her *last chance*. Her school had a strict rule: three tries, and you're out of the nursing program for good.

Most people would have walked away at that point. But not Brooke.

Instead of quitting, she completely changed her approach. She found a tutor, joined a different study group, and shifted from memorizing facts to understanding concepts. She created visual diagrams, taught concepts to her younger sister, and met with her professor during every office hour. She even wrote reminders on sticky notes, such as *"You were made for this."*

On her third try, Brooke passed—with a C. And that C meant *everything*. It wasn't just a grade—it was proof that she didn't give up on herself. That she kept going when most would have stopped.

Brooke's determination with Pathophysiology became a defining moment in her life. Though nursing school ultimately proved too challenging for her testing abilities, that experience of refusing to quit, of changing her approach, of getting back up twice—those lessons shaped everything that came after. She learned that sometimes determination isn't about achieving the original dream; it's about developing the strength to pivot when necessary and find new paths forward.

Today, Brooke uses the resilience she built during those nursing school years in a different career entirely. She often says that learning to persist through Pathophysiology taught her more about her own capabilities than any success ever could have.

Brooke's story illustrates something crucial about determination: it's not about never falling down, and it's not even about achieving your original goal. It's about developing the muscle of persistence that serves you throughout life, regardless of where that life takes you.

Your Determination Action Plan

Now that you understand what real determination looks like, here's how to build it into your daily life:

Week 1: Assessment and Foundation

- Identify one goal you've been avoiding because it feels too challenging
- Break that goal into smaller, manageable steps
- Create a support system by telling three people about your commitment
- Design your environment to support persistence (remove distractions, set up helpful resources)

Week 2: Building Systems

- Establish daily routines that move you toward your goal
- Practice the "2-minute rule"—commit to working on your goal for just 2 minutes daily

- Start a progress journal to track efforts and lessons learned

- Seek feedback from someone who has achieved what you're working toward

Week 3: Handling Setbacks

- Expect and plan for obstacles—what will you do when things get difficult?

- Practice reframing challenges as information rather than judgment

- Develop your "why"—write down why this goal matters to you

- Create a list of small rewards for persistent effort

Week 4: Building Momentum

- Increase your daily commitment time as 2 minutes becomes easy

- Share a progress update with your support system

- Help someone else who's working toward a similar goal

- Plan your next 30-day determination challenge

The Compound Effect of Determination

Here's what I've observed from years of mentoring determined young women: determination creates a compound effect that extends far beyond any single goal.

When you develop the ability to persist through challenges in one area, that capacity transfers to every other area of your life. The determination you build studying for a difficult exam helps you persist through relationship challenges. The grit you develop learning a new skill helps you navigate career setbacks. The resilience you build facing one disappointment gives you strength to handle whatever comes next.

Brooke's experience with Pathophysiology didn't lead to her becoming a nurse, but it taught her something equally valuable: that she could handle difficulty, that she could change her approach when something wasn't working, and that her worth wasn't determined by any single outcome. Those lessons now serve her in every challenge she faces.

Alessia, the aspiring doctor I mentioned at the beginning of this chapter, didn't just learn to handle medical school rejection. She learned that she could handle any setback by treating it as information rather than judgment, by getting curious instead of defeated, by adjusting her approach instead of abandoning her dreams.

The Ripple Effects of Your Determination

Your determination doesn't just change your life—it changes the lives of everyone who witnesses it.

When you persist through challenges, you give other young women permission to do the same. When you get back up after failure, you show others that setbacks aren't permanent. When you achieve goals that once seemed impossible, you expand what others believe is possible for themselves.

Every time you choose determination over defeat, you're not just building your own future—you're building a future where more young women believe in their ability to overcome obstacles and achieve their dreams.

Your Determined Future Starts Now

Determination isn't a trait you're born with—it's a skill you develop through practice, perspective, and persistence. It's not about never facing obstacles; it's about never letting obstacles have the final word.

And sometimes, determination looks different than we expect. Sometimes it means pivoting when a path isn't working. Sometimes it means finding value in efforts that didn't lead to our original goals. Sometimes it means recognizing that the strength we built pursuing one dream becomes the foundation for achieving another.

The challenges you're facing right now aren't evidence that you're on the wrong path. They're evidence that you're developing capabilities you'll need throughout life. The setbacks you encounter aren't signs to give up—they're opportunities to build resilience that will serve you in ways you can't yet imagine.

Every determined woman who came before you—from Marie Curie to Malala, from J.K. Rowling to the students I mentor today—faced moments when their original plans didn't work out. What separated them wasn't the absence of obstacles or the achievement of every goal they set, but their refusal to let setbacks define their possibilities.

Your determination begins with a choice. Not a choice to achieve every dream exactly as you first imagined it, but a choice to keep growing, learning, and moving forward regardless of how your path evolves.

The world needs the strength you're building. It needs your adaptability, your persistence, and your refusal to accept that setbacks mean failure.

So when the next challenge comes—and it will—remember Brooke, remember Alessia, remember every woman who chose to find value and strength in difficulty, regardless of the final outcome.

Your growth is counting on your determination. Don't let it down.

In our final chapter, we'll explore how to integrate everything you've learned—being bold, ambitious, and determined—into a comprehensive approach for building the career and life you want. But everything we build going forward rests on this foundation: your commitment to persist through challenges until you achieve what you're meant to achieve.

Your determined journey starts now. What will you refuse to give up on?

73

Chapter 6
Stand Up for Yourself & Others

The meeting room went silent, and I could feel every eye in the room turn toward me.

I was 28 years old, the only woman in a leadership meeting at a major consulting firm in London, presenting a strategy that could save the company millions. But my colleague James had just interrupted me mid-sentence for the third time, essentially repeating my ideas as if they were his own.

The familiar voice in my head whispered: "Just let it go. Don't make waves. Stay quiet and professional."

But another voice—stronger, clearer—spoke up: "This ends now."

I took a breath, looked directly at James, and said with calm authority: "James, I'd like to finish my point. As I was saying..." Then I turned to the room and continued my presentation.

The shift was immediate. Not just in that meeting, but in how my colleagues treated me from that day forward. By refusing to be invisible, I had changed the entire dynamic.

That moment taught me something crucial about standing up for yourself: it's not about being aggressive or confrontational. It's about having enough respect for your own value to ensure others respect it too.

The High Cost of Playing Small

Here's what happens when brilliant young women consistently refuse to stand up for themselves: they become invisible in their own lives. Their ideas get attributed to others. Their boundaries get trampled. Their potential gets wasted.

Standing up for yourself means refusing to play small. It's saying "no" when others expect you to say "yes," calling out unfairness—even if your voice shakes—and not apologizing for being ambitious, opinionated, or different. It's about owning your space in rooms where you were never meant to blend in.

Most importantly: it's not about being rude. It's about being honest, brave, and unapologetically yourself.

You deserve to be heard and respected. Whether it's in school, at work, or in your personal life, you have the right to stand up for yourself and others. You are your best advocate—and sometimes, you're the only advocate you have.

Before we dive into how to develop this crucial skill, think about your own relationship with self-advocacy:

- When was the last time you let someone else take credit for your ideas or work? How did that feel?

- What situations make you most likely to stay silent when you should speak up?

- What fears hold you back from standing up for yourself— and are those fears actually realistic?

- Who in your life models healthy self-advocacy? What can you learn from their approach?

Now, let's explore why standing up for yourself matters more than ever—and how to do it effectively.

Why Self-Advocacy Is Career Insurance

Standing up for oneself is crucial for several reasons:

Self-Respect and Confidence

Every time you advocate for yourself, you're sending a message—to others and to yourself—that your needs, ideas, and boundaries matter. This isn't just feel-good psychology; it's practical career strategy. When you consistently stand up for yourself, you build a reputation as someone who knows their worth and won't be taken advantage of.

Career Advancement

In my years of international recruiting and team building, I've observed a clear pattern: the professionals who advance fastest aren't necessarily the most technically skilled—they're the ones who consistently advocate for their contributions, negotiate for better opportunities, and ensure their achievements are visible.

Self-advocacy directly impacts:

- Salary negotiations and promotion discussions

- Assignment of high-visibility projects

- Recognition for your contributions

- Leadership opportunities

- Professional reputation and respect

Equality and Fairness

When you stand up for yourself, you're not just protecting your own interests—you're contributing to a more equitable environment for everyone. Every time you refuse to accept unfair treatment, you make it easier for the next woman to do the same.

Unfortunately, workplace equality isn't automatic—it requires active participation from those who experience inequality.

Understanding the gender pay gap is crucial for effective self-advocacy because it reveals exactly where and why women need to negotiate more strategically.

The gender pay gap—a persistent reality across industries and countries—stems from several interconnected factors that self-advocacy can directly address:

- **Occupational Segregation:** Women remain concentrated in traditionally lower-paying industries and roles, often due to cultural expectations about "appropriate" careers for women. Even when women enter higher-paying fields like technology or finance, they're frequently steered toward support roles rather

76

than leadership or technical positions that command higher salaries.

- **Work Experience Disparities:** Women's career trajectories are often interrupted by caregiving responsibilities, resulting in fewer years of continuous experience compared to male counterparts. However, this gap is often used to justify lower compensation even when women return with enhanced skills like project management, multitasking, and crisis resolution developed through caregiving roles.

- **Systemic and Unconscious Bias:** Subtle discrimination affects performance evaluations, promotion decisions, and salary determinations. Studies show that identical resumes receive different responses depending on whether they carry traditionally male or female names. Women's achievements are more likely to be attributed to luck or team effort, while men's successes are credited to individual skill and leadership.

- **Negotiation Pattern Differences:** Women negotiate less frequently for initial salaries and raises, often due to cultural conditioning that frames self-advocacy as unfeminine or aggressive. When women do negotiate, they face social penalties that men don't encounter, creating a double bind that requires more sophisticated negotiation strategies.

These factors compound over time, creating significant lifetime earning disparities that self-advocacy skills can help address. Understanding these systemic issues empowers you to negotiate more strategically and advocate for compensation that reflects your true value.

Here's something that can immediately impact your earning potential:

In most U.S. states, employers cannot legally ask about your current salary during the hiring process. This law exists to prevent wage discrimination from following you from job to job. Know your rights: the compensation should be based on the role's requirements and your qualifications, not your previous pay.

If asked about salary history, you can respond: "I'd prefer to focus on the value I can bring to this role. What's the budgeted range for this position?"

Setting Boundaries

Boundaries aren't walls—they're guidelines that help others understand how to treat you respectfully. When you clearly communicate your limits and consistently enforce them, you create healthier relationships and more productive work environments.

The Cultural Programming We Need to Overcome

The reason young women struggle with self-advocacy isn't personal weakness—it's cultural programming. From early childhood, girls receive different messages than boys about how to behave, what's acceptable, and what makes them "likeable."

This connects to a pattern we explored in our determination chapter: men typically apply for jobs when they meet about 60% of qualifications, while women typically apply only when they meet 100%. This difference in application behavior directly impacts self-advocacy because it reflects the same underlying conditioning that makes women hesitant to speak up for themselves in other professional situations.

The hesitation to apply unless fully qualified mirrors the hesitation to negotiate salaries, request promotions, or advocate for recognition. Both behaviors stem from the same cultural programming that teaches women to be absolutely certain before taking action, while men are encouraged to be confident even in uncertainty.

This pattern shows up consistently across professional situations: women wait until they feel completely prepared to speak up, while men are more likely to advocate for themselves based on potential rather than proven qualifications. Understanding this connection helps explain why developing self-advocacy skills requires intentional practice—you're working against years of conditioning that taught you to wait for permission rather than create opportunities.

How Boys and Girls Are Raised Differently

Expectations: Boys are typically encouraged to be assertive, take risks, and compete. Girls are encouraged to be helpful, agreeable, and avoid conflict.

Role Models: Boys see more examples of male leaders across industries, while girls have fewer visible examples of women in positions of power.

Feedback: Girls get praised for being "good" and "nice," while boys get rewarded for being bold and taking initiative.

The result? Many brilliant young women enter adulthood believing that:

- Asking for what they want is selfish

- Disagreeing with authority is disrespectful

- Standing up for themselves makes them "difficult"

- Their worth comes from being helpful rather than effective

It's time to reprogram these limiting beliefs.

Your Self-Advocacy Toolkit: Practical Strategies That Work

1. Speak Up Strategically

Voicing your opinions isn't about talking more—it's about speaking with purpose and authority when it matters.

In meetings and classes:

- Prepare key points in advance so you can contribute confidently

- Use phrases like "I have a different perspective" or "Here's another approach to consider"

- Don't apologize for having opinions: say "I think..." not "I'm sorry, but I think..."

In social settings:

- Share your genuine thoughts instead of agreeing to keep peace

- Ask questions that advance the conversation

- Don't minimize your expertise or experiences

2. Set and Maintain Clear Boundaries

Boundaries are your responsibility to communicate and enforce. You can't expect others to respect limits they don't know exist.

Professional boundaries:

- "I'm not available for work emails after 7 PM"

- "I need advance notice for overtime requests"

- "Let's keep our discussion focused on the project requirements"

Personal boundaries:

- "I'm not comfortable with that topic of conversation"

- "I need some space to think about this decision"

- "I don't discuss my personal relationships at work"

3. Master Assertive Communication

Assertiveness is the sweet spot between passive and aggressive communication. It's clear, respectful, and firm.

The assertiveness formula:

1. State the facts without emotion

2. Express your feelings or needs

3. Request specific action

4. Explain the benefit or consequence

Example: "When my ideas are presented by others without credit (fact), I feel undervalued (feeling). I need recognition for my contributions (request). This will help me continue bringing my best work to the team (benefit)."

4. Build Your Advisory Network

Self-advocacy is easier when you have experienced guides who can help you navigate challenging situations and build your confidence.

Seek mentors who:

- Model healthy self-advocacy in their own careers

- Can provide specific guidance for your industry or field

- Will give you honest feedback about your communication style

- Support your growth without trying to change your personality

5. Develop Strategic Negotiation Skills

Negotiation isn't about getting everything you want—it's about finding mutually beneficial solutions while ensuring your needs are met.

Preparation is key:

- Research market rates for salaries and benefits

- Document your achievements and contributions

- Identify your non-negotiables and areas where you can be flexible

- Practice your key points beforehand

During negotiations:

- Focus on value you bring, not personal financial needs

- Use collaborative language: "How can we make this work for both of us?"

- Be prepared to walk away if terms aren't acceptable

6. Curate a Circle That Supports Your Growth

The people around you significantly influence your willingness to advocate for yourself. Choose relationships that encourage your authenticity rather than your compliance.

Build relationships with people who:

- Celebrate your successes without minimizing them

- Encourage you to pursue opportunities even when you're nervous

- Give you honest feedback about situations where you should speak up

- Model healthy self-advocacy in their own lives

Learning from Women Who Changed the Game

Sheryl Sandberg: As former COO of Meta, Sheryl consistently advocated not just for herself but for systemic changes that benefit all women in the workplace. Her "Lean In" philosophy encourages women to assertively pursue leadership roles and speak up in professional settings.

Susan Fowler: When faced with systemic harassment at Uber, Susan documented her experiences and published them publicly. Her courage to speak up led to company-wide changes and increased awareness of workplace harassment across the tech industry.

Tarana Burke: The founder of the #MeToo movement demonstrated how individual self-advocacy can become a global movement for change. Her willingness to share her story created space for millions of women to speak their truth.

What these women show us: standing up for yourself can start as personal advocacy and evolve into systemic change that benefits countless others.

Real-Life Scenarios: Practicing Self-Advocacy

Let's explore how self-advocacy looks in real situations you might face:

Personal Safety and Boundaries

Trust Your Gut: When someone pressures you into something that doesn't feel right—whether it's at a party, in a relationship, or in any social situation—your discomfort is valid information. Trust it.

Instead of worrying about their reaction, take a breath and say clearly: "No, I'm not comfortable with that." Your safety and comfort matter more than anyone else's approval.

Protect Your Future: In relationships and intimate situations, remember that your body, your health, and your future are yours to protect. Anyone who truly cares about you will respect your boundaries without argument.

If someone pressures you to take risks you're not comfortable with, you can say: "If you care about me, you'll respect my choices." Anyone who doesn't respect this response has shown you exactly who they are.

Speak Up When Something Feels Wrong: If an adult or authority figure treats you inappropriately—whether through words, actions, or behavior that makes you uncomfortable— speaking up isn't disrespectful. It's necessary.

Find a trusted adult and report what happened. Your safety matters more than anyone's reputation or feelings. Sometimes the bravest thing you can do is say, "This isn't okay," even when it feels scary.

Your Choices Are Yours: Adults may try to influence your decisions about education, career, relationships, or life goals based on their own beliefs or experiences. While input can be valuable, remember that you're the one who has to live with the consequences of your choices.

You deserve respect for your decisions, not judgment. Your path doesn't have to look like anyone else's to be valid.

Be Authentic with Your Emotions: You don't owe anyone fake enthusiasm, forced smiles, or pretend agreement. It's okay to say "I'm not feeling up for this" or "I disagree with that approach."

Your authentic feelings and reactions are valid. Don't sacrifice your emotional honesty to make others more comfortable.

Challenge Harmful Traditions: Just because something has "always been done" doesn't make it right. If family, cultural, or social traditions feel harmful or limiting to you, you have the right to question them.

You can respectfully say: "I understand this is traditional, but it doesn't align with my values" or "I'm choosing a different path for myself."

Ignore the Labels: When you stand up for yourself, some people may call you "difficult," "bossy," or "dramatic." These labels are often used to silence women who refuse to accept unfair treatment.

Remember: standing up for yourself doesn't make you difficult—it makes you someone who knows their worth. The world needs more women who refuse to accept less than they deserve.

Self-Advocacy in Action: Real Stories

Let's look at how self-advocacy plays out in real situations:

Story 1: The Sleepover Decision

Samantha had been looking forward to Mia's birthday sleepover for weeks. But when she arrived, Mia's older brother and his friends were hanging around, teasing the girls and daring them to sneak out of the house late at night.

Samantha's stomach tightened. She didn't like it. It didn't feel safe.

The other girls giggled nervously, but Samantha stood up and said, "I'm not sneaking out. It's not worth getting into trouble or risking something bad happening."

Even though a few girls rolled their eyes, others stood with her.

They stayed inside, made popcorn, and had way more fun safely.

Lesson: Being the first to say "no" isn't easy, but it gives others permission to make safe choices too.

Story 2: The Group Project

Lily was excited to work on a group project in history class—until she realized she was doing all the work while the others texted on their phones.

She didn't want to seem mean, but she didn't want to let herself be walked on.

At the next meeting, she calmly said, "I need help. This is a group project, and it's not fair if I do everything. Can we split it up?"

The others grumbled but agreed.

Lesson: Speaking up respectfully about unfair situations doesn't make you difficult—it makes you someone who values fairness.

Story 3: The Outfit Pressure

At the mall, Julia's friends kept daring her to buy a top she didn't feel comfortable wearing. "Come on, you'll look hot!" they teased.

Julia looked in the mirror. It wasn't her.

She smiled and shook her head. "Nah, that's not my style. I want to wear what feels like me."

Her friends laughed but also respected her more because she didn't cave in.

Lesson: You don't have to follow the crowd. Being true to yourself is always cooler than fitting in.

Story 4: The Secret

Marion's cousin told her something scary about an adult in their family who had made her feel uncomfortable.

Marion felt sick to her stomach. Part of her wanted to pretend she hadn't heard it.

But she remembered: If something feels wrong, staying silent helps no one.

Marion told her mom, who immediately made sure her cousin was safe.

Lesson: Being brave sometimes means saying something even when it's hard. Speaking up can change someone's life.

Story 5: The First Job Interview

Ava landed an interview at a trendy boutique. The manager told her, "You'll need to work extra hours whenever we say—no complaints—and you won't be paid overtime."

Ava felt her cheeks burn. She needed the job badly. But she also knew being desperate didn't mean accepting mistreatment.

She smiled and said, "Thank you for the opportunity, but I believe in fair pay for fair work. I'll have to pass."

As she left, her heart raced with pride.

Lesson: Know your worth—and walk away when someone doesn't respect it.

Story 6: The Party Picture

At a friend's party, some older guys handed Emma a drink and snapped pictures of her holding it, even though she wasn't drinking.

Later, she saw the pictures posted online with captions that made it seem like she was partying hard.

Her stomach sank.

Instead of staying quiet, Emma texted the poster directly: "Take the photos down now. You're posting lies, and it's affecting my reputation."

They deleted the pictures.

Lesson: Never be afraid to demand respect for your name and reputation.

Story 7: The "Just One Hit" Pressure

Sophia was out with coworkers after her first week at her new job. Someone pulled out a vape pen and passed it around.

"Come on, it's just one hit. Everyone's doing it."

Sophia shook her head, laughing lightly. "I don't care what everyone's doing—I like being the one who doesn't."

They teased her for a minute, but by the next week, two coworkers pulled her aside and said they wished they'd said "no."

Lesson: The strongest person in the room isn't always the loudest—it's often the one who quietly says "no."

Story 8: The Relationship Red Flag

Maya's new boyfriend would get jealous when she spent time with friends.

At first, she thought it was cute. But then he started texting nonstop: *Where are you? Who are you with?*

One night, after getting twenty angry texts in a row, Maya finally said to herself, "Love isn't supposed to feel like fear."

She sat him down and said, "I won't be in a relationship where trust is missing. I'm choosing myself."

She walked away.

Lesson: Choosing yourself over an unhealthy relationship isn't selfish—it's self-preservation.

Story 9: The "Be a Good Girl" Pressure

Natalie was a hostess at a restaurant when a customer started making inappropriate comments.

Her manager said, "Just smile and deal with it. Don't make a scene."

Natalie froze for a moment but then stood taller.

"I'm here to do my job, not be harassed. I'm asking you to back me up."

When the manager didn't, she documented the incident, reported it to HR, and found another job where the leadership cared about their people.

Lesson: "Good girls" don't have to accept harassment. Demand respect and find environments that support you.

Story 10: The Friend Who Crossed the Line

Layla's best friend started sharing private things Layla had trusted her with—things she never wanted to be public.

At first, Layla tried to ignore it, afraid of losing the friendship.

But finally, she said, "Friends don't use my secrets for laughs. That hurt me. I deserve better."

It was awkward and painful, but Layla realized: Real friends don't make you feel small.

And if they walk away? Good. They made space for real ones to enter.

Lesson: Real friends respect your boundaries. If they don't, they weren't real friends to begin with.

Standing Up for Others: The Ripple Effect

The Day Sydney Spoke Up for Another

Sydney was the kind of student who had many friends. She got along with different groups and enjoyed middle school life. But one day after school at the basketball court, she saw something that stopped her.

A group of boys was laughing at a quiet girl who usually kept to herself. They were teasing her because she wasn't wearing brand-name clothes.

"What are you wearing?"

"Can your family not afford real shoes?"

They said it loud enough for others to hear, hoping to get laughs.

But Sydney didn't laugh.

She felt anger rising in her chest—not just for the cruelty of the comments, but because no one else was saying anything. So, she stepped forward.

"There's no need to be mean to someone," she said, firmly. "Why does it even matter what brand her clothes are? You're being cruel for no reason."

The boys didn't know how to respond. They shuffled away, embarrassed that someone had challenged them in front of their peers.

The girl didn't say much at that moment; her eyes were teary, and her voice was soft, but she gave Sydney a grateful smile that said everything.

That day, Sydney learned that standing up for what's right sometimes means standing alone. But it's always worth it.

When you stand up for others, you're not just protecting them—you're creating a culture where standing up becomes normal instead of exceptional.

Your Self-Advocacy Journey Starts Now

Standing up for yourself and others is essential for achieving equality, respect, and success. The cultural conditioning that taught you to be "nice" over being authentic wasn't designed to serve your best interests—it was designed to keep you quiet and compliant.

But you have the power to rewrite that programming.

Every time you speak up in a meeting, set a boundary in a relationship, or advocate for fair treatment, you're not just protecting yourself—you're making it easier for every woman who comes after you.

Your voice matters. Your boundaries matter. Your dreams and ambitions matter.

The world needs women who know their worth and aren't afraid to demand that others recognize it too. It needs women who will stand up not just for themselves, but for those who haven't found their voice yet.

In our next chapter, we'll explore how to integrate everything you've learned—being bold, ambitious, determined, and willing to stand up for yourself—into a comprehensive approach for building the life and career you deserve.

But it all starts here: with the decision to stop playing small and start taking up the space you've always deserved.

Your voice is powerful. It's time to use it.

Chapter 7
Embrace Confidence

I was sitting in the executive boardroom of a Fortune 500 company in Dubai, the youngest person at the table by fifteen years, the only woman in a room of twelve senior leaders, presenting a market expansion strategy that could make or break a $50 million investment.

Halfway through my presentation, the CEO interrupted me with a question that wasn't really a question: "Are you sure you have enough experience to be making recommendations of this magnitude?"

The room went silent. Every eye was on me. I could feel the weight of that moment—not just for my career, but for every young woman who would sit in a similar chair after me.

I paused, looked him directly in the eye, and said: "I'm sure I have the right analysis and the strategic insight you need to make this decision successfully. My age isn't relevant to the quality of my work."

Then I continued my presentation.

That moment taught me something crucial about confidence: it's not about never feeling nervous or questioned. It's about refusing to let those feelings stop you from occupying the space you've earned.

The Confidence Paradox That Holds Women Back

Here's what nobody tells you about confidence: it's not a feeling you wait for—it's a decision you make. And for young women, that decision is complicated by a cultural paradox that doesn't affect men in the same way.

We're told to be confident, but not too confident. Assertive, but not aggressive. Strong, but still likeable. The result? Many brilliant women spend their energy managing how others perceive their confidence instead of simply being confident.

Confidence is the belief in your abilities and self-worth, but it's also the decision to act on that belief even when you don't feel 100% certain. It plays a significant role in personal and professional success, influencing not just how others perceive you, but how you show up for yourself.

For young women especially, embracing confidence means learning to navigate workplace dynamics, speak up in rooms where you might be the only woman, and advocate for yourself without apologizing for your ambitions.

Before we explore how to build authentic confidence, consider your own relationship with self-assurance:

- Have you ever felt like you didn't belong somewhere, even though you clearly earned your spot?

- What situations make you shrink or stay silent when you should speak up?

- Think of someone whose confidence you admire—what specifically do they do differently?

- If you had 10% more confidence tomorrow, what would you do that you're not doing today?

Now, let's talk about building the kind of confidence that serves you—and changes how the world responds to you.

Impostor Syndrome: The Confidence Thief

Here's what I've learned from mentoring accomplished women across different industries: even the most successful among them battle a persistent inner voice that questions their right to success. That voice has a name—impostor syndrome—and it's particularly loud for women who dare to be ambitious.

Impostor syndrome is the fear of being perceived as less capable than you actually are. It's the voice that whispers "You don't belong here" right when you're about to shine, or "Who do you think you are?" when you're considering a bold move.

But here's the truth that voice doesn't want you to know: you didn't get where you are by accident.

You earned your spot by showing up, working hard, and refusing to settle. You earned it by choosing to be bold, ambitious, and determined when playing small would have been safer. You earned it by developing skills, taking risks, and proving your capabilities over and over again.

Impostor syndrome tries to keep you small, quiet, and doubting yourself. It wants to prevent you from stepping into the greatness that's already yours.

Don't let it win.

Here's how you fight back:

Call it out: When you hear that voice, name it immediately: "That's impostor syndrome talking, not reality." Don't let it take root in your mind.

Stack the evidence: Keep a record of your achievements, positive feedback, and growth moments. When doubt creeps in, you have concrete proof that you deserve your success.

Share your experience: Talk to someone you trust about these feelings. You'll discover that even the most confident women you know have battled similar doubts.

Own your space: You don't need permission to occupy the space you've earned. Speak with authority, contribute your ideas, and act like you belong—because you do.

Reframe the narrative: When impostor syndrome says, "You're not ready," respond with "I'm ready enough, and I'm committed to continuous growth."

Remember: confidence doesn't mean you never feel uncertain. It means you refuse to let uncertainty stop you from taking action.

You are capable, qualified, and have every right to be exactly where you are—and to reach even higher.

Building Authentic Confidence: A Strategic Approach

Confidence isn't built through positive thinking alone—it's built through consistent actions that prove to yourself what you're capable of achieving.

1. Master Your Internal Dialogue

The conversation you have with yourself sets the tone for everything else. Instead of waiting for confidence to feel natural, start practicing confident self-talk.

Replace limiting thoughts:

- Instead of "I can't do this" → "I'm learning how to do this"

- Instead of "I don't know enough" → "I know enough to get started, and I'll learn more along the way"

- Instead of "What if I fail?" → "What if I succeed? And if I don't, what will I learn?"

2. Build Momentum Through Strategic Wins

Confidence grows through evidence of your capabilities. Create opportunities to prove to yourself what you can accomplish.

Start with manageable challenges that stretch you slightly:

- If public speaking intimidates you, begin by asking thoughtful questions in meetings

- If leadership feels overwhelming, volunteer to coordinate a small project

- If networking seems impossible, start by reaching out to one new person each week

Each small victory builds evidence that you can handle bigger challenges.

3. Maintain the Foundation That Supports Confidence

Physical and mental well-being directly impact your ability to show up confidently. When you feel strong physically, it's easier to feel strong mentally.

Prioritize:

- Regular physical activity that makes you feel capable and energized

- Adequate sleep that supports clear thinking and emotional regulation

- Nutrition that fuels sustained energy throughout demanding days

- Stress management techniques that help you stay centered during pressure

4. Invest in Competence-Based Confidence

The most sustainable confidence comes from actual competence. Continuously developing your skills creates genuine reasons to feel confident about your abilities.

Strategies for continuous learning:

- Take courses that directly advance your career goals

- Attend workshops and conferences in your field

- Read extensively about industry trends and best practices

- Seek stretch assignments that force you to develop new capabilities

- Find ways to teach others what you've learned—teaching solidifies knowledge

5. Use Professional Presentation as a Confidence Tool

Your appearance communicates before you even speak. Dressing professionally isn't about vanity—it's about sending clear signals about how you want to be perceived and treated.

My mother, Beryl, always told me to overdress, especially when I wasn't sure of the dress code. Always better to overdress than underdress. She also specified that in social settings, you should either show your legs or a hint of cleavage, but **never both** simultaneously. Having both is an invitation for unwanted attention.

I have lived by this advice, and it has always reflected positively on me.

Professional Interview Attire Guidelines

For professional interviews, your attire should communicate competence, attention to detail, and respect for the opportunity:

Blouse or Dress Shirt: Choose modest blouses or dress shirts in neutral or soft colors. Avoid overly bright patterns that could be distracting.

Blazer: A well-fitted blazer immediately elevates any outfit and communicates professionalism.

Skirt or Dress Pants: Choose knee-length skirts or well-tailored dress pants in solid colors. Ensure they're comfortable and properly fitted.

Suit Options: Tailored suits are always appropriate, especially for formal business environments.

Footwear: Comfortable, closed-toe shoes like flats, loafers, or low-heeled pumps. Avoid casual footwear like sneakers or sandals.

Accessories: Keep jewelry minimal and professional. Avoid anything large or distracting.

Grooming: Ensure all clothing is clean, pressed, and well-fitted. Hair should be neat and professional.

Additional Guidelines:

- Clear or neutral nail polish

- Avoid strong fragrances

- Stick to primary colors: gray, black, or navy blue

The goal is professional polish while remaining comfortable and age-appropriate.

6. Actively Seek Growth Opportunities

Confident people aren't afraid of feedback—they actively seek it because they understand it accelerates growth.

Make feedback productive:

- Ask specific questions: "What's one thing I could improve in my presentations?"

- Request feedback from multiple sources to get comprehensive perspectives

- Thank people for honest feedback, even when it's difficult to hear

- Create action plans based on feedback and follow up on your progress

7. Expand Your Confidence Zone Through Strategic Challenges

Your comfort zone is where confidence goes to die. Growth—and confidence—happen when you consistently take on challenges that stretch your current capabilities.

Approach this strategically:

- Volunteer for projects that require skills you want to develop

98

- Apply for opportunities even when you don't meet every qualification

- Speak up in meetings where your perspective could add value

- Take on leadership roles that push you to coordinate and inspire others

8. Build Momentum Through Recognition

Confident people don't downplay their achievements—they acknowledge them as evidence of their capabilities.

Create systems for celebrating progress:

- Keep a success journal documenting achievements big and small

- Share wins with your support network

- Reward yourself when you hit significant milestones

- Use past successes as evidence when facing new challenges

9. Use Mental Rehearsal to Build Performance Confidence

Your brain doesn't distinguish between vividly imagined experiences and real ones. Visualization literally rewires your neural pathways to support confident performance.

Make visualization specific:

- Picture yourself handling challenging situations with calm competence

- Imagine the details: what you'll say, how you'll stand, how you'll respond to questions

- Visualize positive outcomes and how you'll feel achieving your goals

99

- Use your vision board as a daily reminder of what you're working toward

10. Curate Relationships That Amplify Your Confidence

Confidence is influenced by the people around you. Intentionally build relationships with people who see your potential and encourage your growth.

Seek out:

- Mentors who can guide your development and advocate for opportunities

- Peers who challenge you to think bigger and achieve more

- Champions who celebrate your successes and help you learn from setbacks

- Role models who demonstrate what confident leadership looks like

Confident Communication: Your Professional Superpower

The way you communicate directly impacts how others perceive your confidence and competence. This is especially important for young women entering professional environments where assertive communication might feel unfamiliar or intimidating.

Voice your opinions and ideas confidently in meetings, classrooms, and interviews. Speaking up isn't just about being heard—it's about claiming your rightful place in important conversations.

Mastering Assertive Communication

Assertive communication means expressing your thoughts, feelings, and needs clearly and respectfully—without being aggressive or minimizing yourself to make others comfortable.

It's the balance between standing your ground and respecting others. It's about recognizing that your voice matters just as much as anyone else's.

Key principles:

- You don't have to be loud to be assertive—you just need to be clear
- Confidence isn't about being aggressive or rude
- Your perspective has value and deserves to be heard
- Respectful directness is more effective than passive hints

The more you practice assertive communication, the more natural it becomes. Each time you speak up confidently, you strengthen your reputation as someone whose opinions matter.

Assertive Communication in Action

Here are some ways assertive communication sounds:

Instead of staying silent: "I have a perspective I'd like to share" or "I'd like to add something to this discussion."

Instead of apologizing for boundaries: "I'm not available then. What other times work for the team?" instead of "I'm sorry, but I can't..."

Instead of being interrupted: "I'd like to finish my point" or "Let me complete this thought."

Instead of minimizing your expertise: "Based on my analysis, I recommend..." instead of "I might be wrong, but..."

Instead of overcommitting: "I can't take that on right now" instead of reluctantly agreeing and feeling resentful.

Professional Confidence Strategies

Take Strategic Leadership Opportunities

Leadership experience builds confidence faster than almost anything else. When you successfully guide a project or team, you prove to yourself and others that you can handle responsibility.

Start where you are:

- Volunteer to lead projects at work or school

- Coordinate team initiatives or events

- Mentor newer employees or students

- Take initiative on improvements rather than waiting to be asked

Build Strategic Professional Relationships

Confident professionals understand that success rarely happens in isolation. Building genuine professional relationships creates opportunities, provides support, and expands your influence.

Networking strategies:

- Attend industry events and professional association meetings

- Connect with colleagues across different departments and levels

- Maintain relationships through regular, valuable communication

- Offer help and support to others, not just seek it for yourself

Negotiate with Confidence and Strategy

Negotiation is where confidence directly translates into tangible benefits. Don't shy away from advocating for fair compensation, meaningful responsibilities, and growth opportunities.

Negotiation principles:

- Research market rates and industry standards before any negotiation

- Focus on value you bring, not personal financial needs

- Prepare specific examples of your contributions and achievements

- Remember: letting the other party suggest numbers first often works in your favor

- Practice your key points beforehand so you can speak confidently

Leverage Mentorship for Accelerated Growth

Confident people aren't afraid to learn from others who have achieved what they're working toward. Mentorship relationships provide guidance, perspective, and advocacy.

Finding effective mentors:

- Look for people whose career path or leadership style you admire

- Approach potential mentors with specific requests rather than vague asks for guidance

- Be prepared to act on advice and update mentors on your progress

- Remember that mentorship is a relationship—consider what value you can provide in return

Learning from Confident Trailblazers

Throughout history, confident women have changed the world not because confidence was easy for them, but because they chose to act confidently despite facing significant challenges:

Rosa Parks: Her decision to refuse giving up her bus seat wasn't just an act of defiance—it was an act of profound confidence in the righteousness of her cause. Despite facing arrest, threats, and social pressure, she chose to act on her convictions.

Ada Lovelace: Often considered the first computer programmer, Ada had the confidence to envision possibilities that others couldn't see. Her work on Charles Babbage's analytical engine laid groundwork for modern computing because she believed in ideas that seemed impossible to others.

Eleanor Roosevelt: As First Lady and diplomat, Eleanor transformed what it meant to occupy that role. Her confidence in speaking out on human rights, women's issues, and social justice helped establish the Universal Declaration of Human Rights and redefined what women could achieve in public service.

What these women teach us: confidence isn't the absence of fear or doubt—it's the decision to act according to your values and vision despite those feelings.

A Story of Growing Into Confidence

The Audition That Changed Everything

Cheyenne had a decision to make—follow the crowd or follow her heart.

She was a high school student who loved acting, and when auditions were announced for the school production of *Little Women*, she knew she wanted to try out for Jo—the strong, bold, complex lead. But there was a catch. Two senior girls, both more experienced and well-known in the drama department, were going for the same role. Additionally, Cheyenne was a dedicated athlete on the basketball team, with practices and games demanding her attention every day.

Almost everyone told her to forget it.

"You don't have time."

"You're not going to beat the seniors."

"It's too much for you."

But Cheyenne didn't let the noise drown out her inner voice. Even though she was nervous—terrified, really—she chose to audition anyway. During the tryout, she stumbled over her lines. Her hands shook. She forgot a section. But instead of freezing, she took a deep breath ... and made it up as she went.

She didn't quit. She didn't apologize. She showed up fully with every ounce of courage she had.

And then something amazing happened: she received a call back. And then—she got the part.

Yes, it was one of the most significant roles in the play. Yes, it challenged her in ways she'd never experienced before. But Cheyenne stepped into it with the kind of quiet confidence that says: I may not have it all figured out, but I believe in myself enough to grow into this.

That's what confidence looks like. It's not about having all the answers. It's about showing up anyway—and trusting that you're capable of more than others (or even you) think.

Cheyenne's story illustrates something crucial: confidence isn't about being the most qualified person in the room. It's about believing in your ability to rise to challenges and grow into opportunities.

Your Confident Future Starts Now

Embracing confidence is essential for navigating and succeeding in today's world, but it's especially critical for young women who face unique cultural pressures to be modest, agreeable, and self-effacing.

True confidence isn't about arrogance or never feeling uncertain. It's about believing in your capabilities enough to act on your goals, speak up for your ideas, and pursue opportunities even when you don't feel completely ready.

The strategies we've explored—from managing impostor syndrome to mastering assertive communication to building competence-based confidence—are tools for creating the kind of self-assurance that opens doors and creates opportunities.

Every time you choose to speak up in a meeting, negotiate for fair compensation, or pursue a challenging opportunity, you're not just building your own confidence—you're making it easier for every young woman who comes after you.

The world needs your ideas, your leadership, and your unique perspective. But it won't wait for you to feel perfectly confident before claiming your place at the table.

Your confidence journey starts with a single decision: to believe in your right to take up space, contribute your voice, and pursue your ambitions without apology.

The boardrooms, laboratories, startup offices, and leadership positions of the future are waiting for confident women who understand their worth and aren't afraid to demonstrate it.

That woman is you. Step into your confidence. The world is ready for what you have to offer.

Chapter 8
Be Assertive

The email arrived on a Friday afternoon, just as I was preparing to leave the Geneva office for the weekend.

"Due to budget constraints, we'll need to reduce the scope of your market analysis project. Please adjust your timeline to deliver preliminary findings by Monday instead of the comprehensive report we originally discussed."

I stared at my screen, feeling a familiar tug between two responses: the people-pleasing voice that whispered "Just say yes and figure it out over the weekend," and the professional voice that recognized this was an unreasonable request that would compromise the quality of my work.

For years, I would have chosen the first option—worked all weekend, delivered something rushed, and apologized for it not being my best work. But that day, I chose differently.

I picked up the phone and called my project lead.

"I understand budget constraints are a reality," I said. "However, delivering preliminary findings by Monday won't serve the project goals we established. I can provide a focused analysis of the three key markets by Thursday, which would give you actionable insights while maintaining the quality you need for decision-making. Would that timeline work?"

The response was immediate: "Yes, that makes much more sense. Thank you for pushing back on this."

That moment taught me something crucial about assertiveness: it's not about being difficult or confrontational. It's about having enough respect for your work—and your boundaries—to advocate for solutions that serve everyone better.

The Assertiveness Paradox for Young Women

Here's what makes assertiveness particularly challenging for young women: we live in a culture that simultaneously demands we be confident leaders while punishing us when we actually lead. We're told to speak up, but not too loudly. Take charge, but don't be bossy. Have opinions, but don't be difficult.

The result? Many brilliant women spend their energy trying to be assertive in ways that won't upset anyone, which often means being assertive in ways that aren't actually effective.

True assertiveness is more than polite communication—it means expressing your thoughts, feelings, and beliefs directly, honestly, and respectfully. It involves standing up for yourself while respecting others, setting clear boundaries, and effectively communicating your needs and desires.

For young women, assertiveness is about pushing past the cultural pressure to stay quiet, play nice, or always say "yes." It's about using your voice in classrooms, relationships, and workplaces where you've been conditioned to shrink. It's claiming your space, setting boundaries, and saying, "I matter too."

Most importantly: assertiveness isn't about being bossy or aggressive. It's about knowing your worth and speaking up for it.

Before we explore how to develop assertiveness skills, consider your own relationship with speaking up:

- When did you want to say "no" but said "yes" to avoid conflict? How did that feel?

- When have you felt dismissed or unheard? What would you have said if you felt safe to speak up?

- What internal voice stops you from saying what you think or feel? Is that voice actually protecting you, or holding you back?

Now, let's explore why assertiveness is essential for your success—and how to develop it strategically.

Why Assertiveness Is Your Professional Superpower

1. Self-Advocacy That Creates Respect

Assertiveness ensures you're treated fairly and with respect, but more than that—it teaches others how to treat you. When you consistently advocate for yourself professionally, you establish a reputation as someone who values their contributions and won't accept unfair treatment.

2. Clear Communication That Prevents Problems

Assertive communication eliminates the guesswork in professional relationships. Instead of hoping others will recognize your needs or boundaries, you communicate them clearly. This prevents misunderstandings, reduces conflicts, and creates more productive working relationships.

3. Career Advancement Through Visibility

In professional environments, the people who advance aren't always the most talented—they're often the most visible. Assertiveness ensures your contributions are recognized, your ideas are heard, and your career goals are known. This visibility is crucial for converting internships to full-time offers and securing promotions.

4. Professional Credibility and Respect

Assertive professionals earn respect by demonstrating they understand their value and won't compromise their standards. This creates trust—colleagues know you'll speak up if there are problems, advocate for good solutions, and maintain high standards.

5. Boundary Setting That Protects Your Performance

Assertiveness enables you to establish and maintain healthy boundaries that prevent burnout and protect your long-term performance. This includes saying no to unreasonable requests, advocating for realistic timelines, and communicating your capacity honestly.

(Note: I prefer the term "work-life blend" over "work-life balance," as it's difficult in today's world to keep these areas completely separate, especially when you're passionate about your career. The goal is integration that serves both your professional growth and personal well-being.)

Learning Assertiveness: A Strategic Approach

Assertiveness is a learnable skill that improves with practice and strategic application:

1. Understand the Assertiveness Spectrum

Assertiveness exists on a spectrum between passivity and aggression. Understanding this spectrum helps you find the right approach for different situations:

- **Passive**: Avoiding conflict, not expressing needs, letting others make decisions

- **Assertive**: Clear communication, respectful boundaries, collaborative problem-solving

- **Aggressive**: Demanding, dismissive of others' needs, creating conflict

The goal is assertive communication that's respectful and transparent without being submissive or aggressive.

2. Develop Self-Awareness Around Your Non-Negotiables

Before you can advocate for yourself effectively, you need to understand what matters most to you. This clarity becomes especially crucial when evaluating job offers or negotiating workplace conditions.

When you do get your first job offer, it's tempting to say "yes" right away. You feel excited, validated, and maybe even a little desperate to prove you're worth hiring. But let me tell you a story about Mia—a recent college grad who learned the power of knowing her non-negotiables.

Scene: Mia is sitting at a café, her phone buzzes. It's a voicemail from the recruiter.

Recruiter (voicemail): "Hi Mia, we're excited to extend an offer for the Marketing Coordinator role! The starting salary is $42,000, and we'd love you to start in the office in two weeks. Let us know if you're ready to move forward!"

Mia was thrilled—but something didn't sit right. She remembered a worksheet she'd done with her mentor titled *"Know Your Non-Negotiables."* It listed her five must-haves in a role:

1. A salary that allowed her to live independently

2. Clear path for growth within 1-2 years

3. A leader who would mentor her, not just manage her

4. A company with a strong mission aligned with her values

5. Flexibility for occasional remote work

Scene: Mia meets with her mentor.

Mentor: "Excitement is good, Mia. But let's compare this offer to your non-negotiables. Does it meet them?"

Mia (hesitant): "Well ... not really. The salary is tight, and the company has a high turnover rate. The hiring manager barely looked me in the eye. And I asked about remote work, and they said, 'We're old school here.'"

Mentor: "Then you already have your answer. Don't abandon your standards just because they said yes."

Mia declined the offer. Scary? Yes. Empowering? Absolutely. Two weeks later, another offer came through—from a company that checked every box. Because she waited and knew her non-negotiables, she didn't settle. She stepped into a role where she could thrive.

Reflection:

- What are *your* non-negotiables in a future job?
- Have you ever said "yes" to something that didn't align with your values? What did you learn?

Additional ways to learn assertiveness:

3. Master "I" Statement Communication

"I" statements are the foundation of assertive communication because they express your perspective without creating defensiveness in others.

Effective "I" statements:

- "I need more information before I can commit to this timeline"
- "I feel overwhelmed when projects are assigned without advance notice"
- "I would like to discuss my role in this project to ensure we're aligned"

Avoid "You" statements that sound accusatory:

- Instead of "You never give me enough time" → "I need advance notice to do my best work"
- Instead of "You always interrupt me" → "I'd like to finish my thought"

4. Use Body Language That Reinforces Your Words

Your physical presence communicates as much as your words. Confident body language reinforces assertive communication.

Key elements of assertive body language:

- **Eye contact**: Maintain steady eye contact to convey confidence and sincerity. Hold eye contact long enough to notice the color of their eyes—this creates connection

- **Handshakes**: Use a firm handshake with your whole hand (not just fingertips). A weak handshake can undermine your message

- **Posture**: Keep your shoulders back and stand tall. Your physical presence should match your verbal confidence

- **Voice**: Speak clearly and at an appropriate volume. Don't end statements with uptalk that makes them sound like questions

5. Master the Art of Strategic "No"

Learning to say "no" respectfully is essential for maintaining boundaries and protecting your capacity for high-priority work.

Effective ways to say "no":

- "I can't take on additional projects right now, but I'm happy to revisit this next month"

- "That doesn't align with my current priorities, but let me suggest another approach"

- "I'm not available for that timeline, but here's what I could do instead"

- "I need to decline this opportunity to maintain the quality of my existing commitments"

Remember: "No" is a complete sentence, but providing brief context can maintain relationships while protecting your boundaries.

6. Invest in Formal Assertiveness Development

Consider structured programs that provide guided practice and feedback in safe environments.

Recommended Resources to Build Your Assertive Communication Skills

Speaking up for yourself is a lifelong superpower—and there are great tools out there to help you strengthen it even more.

Here are resources to continue building your voice, confidence, and communication skills:

Toastmasters International or the Gavel Club for participants under 18 years of age. If you want a supportive space to practice speaking with confidence, these clubs are a great (and affordable) option. You'll get practice in public speaking, leadership, and assertive communication—and meet inspiring people along the way! toastmasters.org

The Assertiveness Workbook by Randy J. Paterson This workbook is packed with exercises to help you speak up more clearly, say "no" when needed, and stand your ground without feeling guilty or aggressive. It's like a mini assertiveness coach you can carry with you. Available on Amazon or in most bookstores.

Coursera: "Interpersonal Communication" Course Want to learn communication skills online (and sometimes for free)? Search for "Assertive Communication" or "Interpersonal Communication" on Coursera. Several great courses teach you how to communicate confidently and respectfully. coursera.org

One of my favorite resources is *Lean In Girls*, a powerful program helping girls get a head start on confidence and leadership. It's a free, research-backed initiative designed for girls aged 11 to 15. Created by the team behind LeanIn.Org, (Sheryl Sandberg's nonprofit), this program empowers girls to embrace their strengths, challenge stereotypes, and build the kind of confidence that lasts. Through a series of interactive, real-talk sessions, girls explore what it means to take risks, lead boldly, and stand up for themselves and others. Lean In Girls isn't about telling girls who to be; it's about helping them discover who they already are and giving them the tools to lead on their terms. Whether it's speaking up in class, standing up to bias, or setting bold goals, this program helps the next generation of girls rewrite the rules—and own their power early.

Lean In Circles (designed primarily for adults and professionals) is a community of other women working toward their goals. Lean In Circles provides a space for practicing speaking up, negotiating, and leading while supporting one another. You don't have to do it alone. leanin.org/circles

She Should Run / Running Start If you dream of leading, changing the world, or just making your voice heard in a big way, check out these leadership programs. They teach young women to speak with strength, advocate for themselves, and confidently lead. sheshouldrun.org | runningstart.org

Remember: Building assertive communication is like building a muscle—the more you practice, the stronger you become. Your voice is powerful. Keep using it. Keep strengthening it. The world needs to hear you.

7. Practice Through Safe Scenario Building

Role-playing different scenarios in low-stakes environments builds your confidence for high-stakes situations.

Practice scenarios:

- Requesting a deadline extension for a reasonable reason
- Asking for clarification when instructions are unclear
- Declining additional work when you're at capacity
- Addressing a colleague who consistently interrupts you
- Negotiating for resources you need to complete a project

8. Develop Internal Support for External Assertiveness

Your internal dialogue directly impacts your ability to be assertive externally. Build confidence through supportive self-talk.

Assertive internal dialogue:

- "My perspective has value and deserves to be heard"
- "I can disagree respectfully while maintaining good relationships"
- "Setting boundaries protects my ability to do good work"
- "I have the right to advocate for fair treatment"

Assertive vs. Pushy: Understanding the Distinction

Understanding the difference between assertive and pushy behavior helps you advocate for yourself effectively without damaging relationships:

Assertive Characteristics:

- **Respectful communication** that honors both your needs and others'
- **Collaborative approach** seeking win-win solutions
- **Confidence** that doesn't diminish others
- **Clear boundaries** communicated with explanation when appropriate

Pushy Characteristics:

- **Aggressive communication** that disregards others' needs
- **Self-centered approach** that prioritizes personal gain over mutual benefit
- **Overbearing behavior** that creates conflict and resistance
- **Demands** without consideration for others' perspectives or constraints

The key difference: assertive people respect others while advocating for themselves; pushy people advocate for themselves at others' expense.

Learning from Assertive Leaders Who Changed the World

Throughout history, women have used assertiveness to create positive change, demonstrating that respectful but firm communication can transform systems:

Rosa Parks: Her refusal to give up her seat wasn't aggressive or loud—it was a quiet, firm assertion of her rights that sparked the Civil Rights Movement. She demonstrated that assertiveness can be calm, dignified, and revolutionary.

Sheryl Sandberg: As former COO of Meta, Sheryl consistently advocated for women's advancement in the workplace. Her "lean in" philosophy encourages assertive career navigation while building systems that support other women's success.

Greta Thunberg: The young climate activist demonstrates how assertive communication can mobilize global action. She speaks directly to world leaders with facts, urgency, and unwavering commitment to her cause.

What these women teach us: assertiveness isn't about volume or aggression—it's about clarity, conviction, and consistent action aligned with your values.

Building Your Assertiveness Skills Through Practice

Start with Low-Stakes Situations

Build your assertiveness muscle in situations where the consequences are minimal:

- Express preferences when making social plans

- Ask for what you need at restaurants or stores
- Share your opinion in casual conversations
- Practice saying "no" to small requests that don't serve you

Prepare for High-Stakes Conversations

For important conversations, preparation reduces anxiety and increases effectiveness:

- Identify your key points in advance
- Practice your language until it feels natural
- Anticipate potential responses and plan your replies
- Role-play with trusted friends or mentors

Learn from Each Assertive Interaction

Regular reflection helps you refine your approach:

- What felt comfortable about being assertive in this situation?
- How did others respond to your assertive communication?
- What would you do differently next time?
- How did assertiveness impact the outcome?

Build Your Assertiveness Support Network

Surround yourself with people who support your growth:

- Mentors who can provide guidance and practice opportunities
- Colleagues who model healthy assertiveness
- Friends who encourage you to speak up for yourself
- Professional coaches or counselors if you need additional support

Real Stories of Assertiveness in Action

Sarah's Story: Speaking Up with Faith

I've always found it easier to remain quiet than to speak, especially when it comes to my faith. But one moment at work changed that for me.

One morning, a coworker walked into the kitchen looking anxious. She said, "If anyone has good vibes or prayers, I could use them. I've got a court hearing tomorrow and I'm nervous."

Everyone offered kind words, but there was a pause. My heart was racing. I felt a nudge—I knew I had something to offer, but it meant stepping out of my comfort zone.

So, I took a deep breath and asked, "Would you mind if I prayed with you?" She looked surprised, smiled, and said, "Yes, please."

To my amazement, a few other women in the kitchen quietly came over. We gathered around her, and I prayed out loud. It wasn't perfect. My voice trembled. But it was real.

That moment could have been awkward. I worried that others might think I was being too forward or pushy. But instead, something beautiful happened: our relationships deepened. We started to look out for each other more. We became a stronger team.

Being assertive isn't always about raising your voice; it's about raising your values when it matters.

Sarah's story illustrates something crucial about assertiveness: it's not about being the loudest voice in the room. Sometimes assertiveness means offering something meaningful when you could easily stay silent.

Your Assertive Future Starts Now

Assertiveness isn't about raising your voice—it's about standing your ground, speaking your truth, and refusing to be silenced when it matters most.

Rosa didn't shout when she refused to give up her seat; she stayed seated with quiet dignity, sparking a movement that changed history. Sheryl leaned into boardrooms and broke barriers, encouraging women everywhere to take their seats at the table and speak with confidence. Greta stood with a sign and spoke truth to world leaders, proving that even one young voice can shake the system when it refuses to be ignored.

These women didn't wait for permission—they stood up, spoke out, and took action. Their assertiveness wasn't about volume—it was about clarity, courage, and conviction.

And so is yours.

Every time you speak up in a meeting, set a boundary in a relationship, or advocate for fair treatment, you're not just protecting yourself—you're modeling for other young women what assertive leadership looks like.

The world needs women who can communicate with clarity, advocate with respect, and lead with conviction. It needs women who understand that assertiveness isn't aggression—it's respect for yourself and others expressed through clear, courageous communication.

Your assertive journey starts with small steps: expressing preferences, asking questions, saying "no" when necessary, and advocating for yourself with the same energy you'd use to advocate for someone you care about.

Because you deserve that same level of care and advocacy—from others, and especially from yourself.

Reflection Questions:

6. Which of the women in this chapter do you relate to most—Rosa, Sheryl, or Greta—and why?

7. What message or issue matters so much to you that you'd be willing to stand alone for it, like Greta did?

8. How can you practice being assertive this week—even in small ways, like asking for what you need or saying "no" without apology?

Journal Prompt:

Write about a situation where you wish you had been more assertive. What stopped you?

Now rewrite the moment with your most confident, clear, and courageous voice taking the lead.

What changes?

Final Thought

Assertiveness isn't about being aggressive—it's about being anchored. Anchored in your values, your truth, and your worth.

Whether you're sitting still like Rosa, taking a seat at the table like Sheryl, or holding a sign like Greta, remember this: the world doesn't change because of silence. It changes when someone like you decides to speak up—and doesn't back down.

Your voice matters. Your boundaries matter. Your values matter.

The world is waiting for your assertive leadership. Don't keep it waiting much longer.

Chapter 9
Develop a Strong Work Ethic

When I was working in Hong Kong as a young branch manager for a recruiting firm, I quickly learned an unspoken rule: no one left until the boss did. This wasn't written in any handbook, but it was understood by everyone in the office.

Most of my colleagues would arrive precisely on time and then watch the clock, waiting for our director to pack up before they could leave. But I realized this created an opportunity to distinguish myself through strategic work ethic.

I started coming in early—not dramatically early, but consistently 30 minutes before official start time. I used that time to prepare for the day, review client files, and plan my priorities. More importantly, I stayed focused and productive throughout the day instead of just putting in face time.

While others were visibly waiting for permission to leave, I was genuinely engaged in completing important work. When the boss finally left at 7 PM, I often had legitimate reasons to stay another hour to finish projects that mattered.

This wasn't about being a workaholic or sacrificing work-life balance—it was about demonstrating genuine commitment to excellence in a culture that valued dedication. The difference was intentionality. I wasn't just staying late to be seen; I was using the time strategically to build relationships, complete high-quality work, and position myself as someone who could be trusted with important responsibilities.

Within eight months, I was promoted to regional manager, largely because I had demonstrated not just competence, but the kind of work ethic that leaders could count on. My early arrival and purposeful late departure had created a reputation for reliability and commitment that opened doors throughout my career.

That experience taught me something crucial: your work ethic creates your professional reputation long before your results do. It's about becoming the person others can't imagine succeeding without.

Why Work Ethic Matters More Than Talent

Here's what I've learned from building teams across different cultures and industries: talent is common, but exceptional work ethic is rare. And in competitive environments, work ethic beats talent when talent doesn't work hard.

A strong work ethic is more than just working long hours—it's about showing up consistently, following through completely, and doing your best work even when no one's watching. For young women carving out their place in competitive environments, it's about building credibility that can't be questioned and earning independence that can't be taken away.

Your work ethic speaks before you even say a word. It tells people whether you can be trusted with important projects, whether you'll follow through on commitments, and whether you have the discipline to achieve long-term goals.

Most importantly: exceptional work ethic isn't about being perfect—it's about being reliable, focused, and consistently excellent in a world where mediocrity has become acceptable.

Before we explore how to develop an exceptional work ethic, consider your current relationship with excellence:

- What daily habits could you build now that will compound into significant advantages for your future self?

- What does "showing up 100%" look like in your current responsibilities?

- When you make commitments, do others count on you to follow through completely?

- How do you maintain standards when work becomes routine or challenging?

- Who in your life demonstrates exceptional work ethic, and what specific behaviors make them stand out?

Now, let's explore how to build the kind of work ethic that creates opportunities rather than just completing tasks.

Building Your Strategic Work Ethic Framework

Work ethic isn't just about working harder—it's about working strategically to build long-term credibility and capability:

1. Set Goals That Drive Daily Excellence

Strong work ethic begins with clarity about what you're working toward. When you understand how your current efforts connect to your future goals, it becomes easier to maintain high standards even during routine tasks.

Effective goal setting for work ethic development:

- Define specific professional and personal objectives that matter to you

- Connect daily tasks to larger purposes so routine work feels meaningful

- Set standards for excellence that exceed minimum requirements

- Create accountability systems that help you maintain consistency

2. Build Systems That Support Excellence

Organization isn't just about keeping track of tasks—it's about creating systems that make high-quality work sustainable and stress-free.

Strategic organization approaches:

- Use planning tools that match your workflow preferences (digital or physical)

- Create systems for tracking both deadlines and quality standards

- Build routines that ensure important tasks get adequate time and attention

- Develop backup plans for when unexpected challenges arise

3. Master Strategic Priority Management

Exceptional work ethic isn't about doing everything—it's about doing the right things exceptionally well. This requires sophisticated priority management that goes beyond basic time management.

To help me prioritize tasks, I use a framework developed by Colin Eden and Fran Ackermann called the "Prioritization Power Grid."

Exercise: The Prioritization Power Grid

Below is a quick way to sort your to-do list using two questions:

1. Is it Important? (Does it help you reach your goals or affect your future?)

2. Is it Urgent? (Does it need to be done now, or is there a deadline soon?)

Step 1: Write down 6–8 things you need to do this week—school, work, chores, personal goals, etc.

Step 2: Use the chart above to place each task in one of the four boxes:

Step 3: Reflect

- Are you spending too much time on "not important" tasks?

- How would your week feel if you focused more on what's truly important?

Reflection Questions:

- Which box do most of your tasks fall into?

- What could you stop doing to free up time for what really matters?

- How does your work ethic change when you plan your week purposefully?

This prioritization framework helps ensure your excellent work ethic is applied to activities that actually advance your goals, not just activities that feel busy.

4. Develop Discipline That Builds Momentum

Discipline isn't about forcing yourself to work—it's about creating sustainable routines that make excellent work feel natural and inevitable.

Building sustainable discipline:

- Create routines that align with your natural energy patterns

- Start with small, consistent habits that build confidence

- Focus on consistency over perfection—daily progress compounds

- Build accountability systems that support your commitment to excellence

5. Develop Initiative That Creates Value

Taking initiative distinguishes exceptional work ethic from merely completing assigned tasks. It shows you're thinking strategically about how to add value beyond basic requirements.

Strategic initiative behaviors:

- Identify problems before they become urgent issues

- Suggest improvements to processes you're involved in

- Volunteer for projects that develop your skills and expand your impact

- Anticipate needs and prepare solutions before being asked

6. Cultivate an Attitude That Inspires Excellence

Your attitude doesn't just affect your own productivity—it influences how others perceive your capabilities and whether they want to work with you on important projects.

Professional attitude behaviors:

- Approach challenges as problems to solve rather than obstacles to endure

- Maintain enthusiasm for projects even when they become routine

- Support team morale through constructive communication and collaborative problem-solving

- View setbacks as learning opportunities that strengthen your capabilities

7. Build Reliability That Creates Trust

Reliability is the foundation of professional reputation. When people know they can count on you to deliver quality work on time, you become someone they turn to for important opportunities.

Reliability building strategies:

- Under-promise and over-deliver consistently

- Communicate proactively if challenges arise that might affect your commitments

- Build buffer time into your planning to ensure you can meet deadlines even when unexpected issues occur

- Keep detailed records of your commitments so nothing falls through the cracks

8. Pursue Continuous Improvement Through Strategic Feedback

Exceptional work ethic includes the humility to seek feedback and the discipline to act on it. This creates a cycle of continuous improvement that compounds over time.

Effective feedback utilization:

- Ask specific questions that help you improve rather than seeking general praise

- Request feedback from multiple sources to get comprehensive perspectives

- Create action plans based on feedback and track your progress implementing changes

- View feedback as investment in your future capabilities rather than criticism of current performance

Making Your Work Ethic Visible and Valued

Having exceptional work ethic isn't enough—you need to ensure it's recognized and valued by people who can create opportunities for you:

1. Communicate Your Excellence Strategically

Keep stakeholders informed about your progress and problem-solving approaches. Regular, professional communication demonstrates your commitment and builds confidence in your capabilities.

Effective communication strategies:

- Provide regular updates that highlight progress and address challenges proactively

- Share your problem-solving process, not just your results

- Communicate timelines and expectations clearly to manage relationships effectively

- Document your contributions so your value is visible to decision-makers

2. Consistently Exceed Quality Expectations

Focus on producing work that exceeds expectations rather than just meeting minimum requirements. High-quality output is the most compelling evidence of exceptional work ethic.

Quality excellence strategies:

- Set personal standards higher than official requirements

- Review your work multiple times before submission

- Seek opportunities to add value beyond basic task completion

- Remember: "under-promise and over-deliver" builds lasting credibility

3. Demonstrate Proactive Problem-Solving

Identify opportunities to add value before being asked. Proactive behavior shows dedication, strategic thinking, and leadership potential.

4. Build a Reputation for Unwavering Consistency

Consistency in meeting or exceeding responsibilities builds a reputation for dependability that creates long-term opportunities.

5. Actively Pursue Growth Opportunities

Express genuine interest in taking on new challenges. This demonstrates ambition, confidence, and commitment to continuous development.

Protecting Your Work Ethic from Exploitation

Strong work ethic can make you a target for people who want to take advantage of your reliability. Learning to protect your standards while maintaining excellence is crucial for long-term success:

1. Set Clear Boundaries That Protect Your Excellence

Communicate your limits professionally and know when to push back on unreasonable requests. People sometimes take advantage of reliable individuals, so you need to recognize when "helpful" becomes "exploitative."

Boundary-setting strategies:

- Distinguish between reasonable requests and attempts to avoid responsibility

- Recognize patterns where others consistently rely on your work without reciprocating

- Protect your integrity by refusing to enable academic dishonesty or workplace shortcuts

- Set limits that prevent burnout while maintaining your reputation for excellence

2. Master Strategic Saying "No" While Maintaining Relationships

Politely decline tasks that exceed your capacity or compromise your ability to deliver excellent work. Protecting your capacity ensures you can maintain high standards on your priority commitments.

3. Document Your Contributions and Capacity

Keep detailed records of your tasks, time investment, and achievements. This helps you manage your workload and provides evidence of your contributions when seeking recognition or advancement.

I strongly suggest keeping a record of your activities while interning, so you can later share your accomplishments with your manager.

4. Address Workload Issues Proactively

When you feel overwhelmed, discuss your workload professionally and seek solutions that maintain your quality standards. Use prioritization frameworks to create shared understanding about what takes precedence.

A strong suggestion is to complete the prioritization grid together, so you are on the same page. With an agreed list, you can easily push back on additional tasks.

The Components of Exceptional Work Ethic

Exceptional work ethic manifests through specific, observable behaviors:

Punctuality: Respecting Time as a Professional Resource

Being consistently on time—or early—for commitments demonstrates reliability and respect for others' time. It's often the first impression people form about your professionalism.

Diligence: Maintaining Standards Regardless of Task Visibility

Putting consistent effort into all tasks, including routine ones, demonstrates commitment to excellence regardless of recognition or oversight.

Accountability: Owning Results and Learning from Setbacks

Taking responsibility for both successes and mistakes indicates integrity and professional maturity that builds trust over time.

Perseverance: Maintaining Excellence Through Challenges

Continuing to deliver quality work despite obstacles demonstrates the resilience and determination that distinguish exceptional professionals.

Teamwork: Contributing to Collective Excellence

Collaborating effectively while maintaining personal standards creates environments where everyone can do their best work.

Adaptability: Maintaining Standards While Embracing Change

Flexibility and openness to new approaches while maintaining quality standards shows you can handle evolving responsibilities effectively.

Work Ethic Traits That Create Career Opportunities

These specific behaviors consistently lead to recognition, advancement, and increased opportunities:

1. Reliability: Building Trust Through Consistent Excellence

Being someone others can count on to deliver quality work on schedule. When you're consistently reliable, people begin to see you as someone who can handle increased responsibility and important projects.

2. Initiative: Creating Value Through Proactive Leadership

Identifying needs and addressing them without being asked. Taking initiative demonstrates leadership potential and strategic thinking that sets you apart from people who only complete assigned tasks.

3. Quality Excellence: Consistently Exceeding Standards

Paying attention to details and maintaining high standards regardless of task significance. Quality work demonstrates pride and professionalism that builds your reputation for excellence.

4. Dependability: Following Through on Every Commitment

Being someone others can count on completely. When you consistently follow through on commitments, people begin to trust you with increasingly important responsibilities.

5. Integrity: Maintaining Standards Regardless of Oversight

Doing excellent work and making ethical choices even when no one is watching. Integrity builds long-term credibility that becomes the foundation of leadership opportunities.

6. Accountability: Learning and Growing from All Outcomes

Taking responsibility for results, learning from mistakes, and using setbacks as opportunities for improvement. Accountability demonstrates maturity and commitment to continuous growth.

7. Consistency: Delivering Excellence as Your Standard Operating Procedure

Maintaining high standards regardless of circumstances, mood, or external pressures. Consistency builds trust and demonstrates that your excellence is dependable, not accidental.

8. Professional Attitude: Approaching Challenges with Solution-Focused Energy

Maintaining constructive, collaborative energy even during difficult projects. Your attitude influences not just your own performance, but the performance of everyone around you.

A Story of Work Ethic That Creates Opportunities

The Power of Discipline: Julia's Story

During my MBA program in London, I met someone who would leave a lasting impression on me, not just because of her intelligence, but because of her work ethic. Her name was Julia.

The program was intense, and out of a cohort of forty students, only six of us were women. It was competitive, challenging, and at times overwhelming. However, Julia stood out from the start.

Every time we worked together, I was amazed by her level of preparation. She didn't just take notes; she created intricate spider diagrams, used colors to organize ideas, and broke down complex topics into visuals that made studying feel possible. Her notebooks looked more like works of art than lecture notes.

But Julia's brilliance didn't stop at the classroom.

When we later worked together on group projects, she was the definition of dependable. She never missed a deadline. She never turned in anything that was only partially done. Julia always gave her best, whether it was a written report or a group presentation. She took pride in her work, not for recognition, but because she believed in doing things well.

To this day, I haven't met many people with her level of dedication and consistency. Any employer would be lucky to have someone like Julia on their team.

She taught everyone around her that talent will take you far, but a strong work ethic will take you further.

Julia's story illustrates something crucial: exceptional work ethic isn't about perfection—it's about consistently applying high standards to everything you do, which creates compound advantages over time.

Your Work Ethic Legacy Starts Now

Exceptional work ethic isn't just about being productive—it's about building a reputation that creates opportunities throughout your career. When people know they can count on you for quality work, professional communication, and reliable follow-through, you become someone they turn to for important projects and advancement opportunities.

Your work ethic speaks for you in rooms where you're not present. It influences whether you get recommended for promotions, invited to join high-visibility projects, or considered for leadership roles.

The habits you build now—showing up early, exceeding expectations, taking initiative, maintaining quality standards—compound into career advantages that distinguish you throughout your professional life.

Every project you approach with excellence, every deadline you meet ahead of schedule, every time you volunteer to solve problems rather than just complete tasks, you're building a foundation of credibility that will support your ambitions for decades.

The world needs women who combine talent with exceptional work ethic, who bring both capability and reliability to important challenges. It needs women who understand that excellence isn't just about personal achievement—it's about creating value that makes everyone around them more successful.

Your exceptional work ethic journey starts with the next task you're given, the next deadline you face, the next opportunity to exceed expectations.

Make your effort speak volumes. Make it say something powerful about who you are and what you're capable of achieving.

Because when your work ethic becomes your calling card, opportunities don't just knock—they seek you out.

Chapter 10
Effective Networking

I was twenty-four years old, attending my first international conference in Frankfurt, when I realized I had made a critical career mistake.

Not in choosing my job or my field, but in believing that exceptional work alone would create opportunities. I had spent three years focused exclusively on delivering outstanding results, assuming that recognition would follow naturally. What I discovered in that conference center changed everything.

During the opening reception, I watched colleagues who were less experienced but more connected land meetings with industry leaders, get invited to exclusive dinner discussions, and secure introductions to potential mentors. Meanwhile, I stood alone by the bar, technically qualified to be in every one of those conversations, but professionally invisible.

That night, I made a decision that would transform my career trajectory: I would master the art of strategic relationship building.

Over the next three days, I introduced myself to fifteen people. I asked thoughtful questions, shared my perspectives on industry challenges, and followed up with personalized messages afterward. Six months later, three of those connections had led to new project opportunities, one had become an ongoing mentor, and two had referred me for positions I never would have known existed.

That experience taught me something crucial about professional success: your network isn't just who you know—it's who knows what you're capable of achieving.

The Strategic Power of Professional Relationships

Networking isn't about collecting business cards or manipulating people into helping you—it's about building genuine relationships with people who inspire, support, and challenge you to grow. For young women entering competitive professional environments, strategic networking means creating a foundation of relationships before you desperately need them.

The most successful professionals understand something that school rarely teaches: opportunities flow through relationships. The internship that launches your career, the mentor who opens doors, the peer who recommends you for a promotion—these connections happen because someone who knows your capabilities thinks of you when opportunities arise.

Whether you're attending events, joining organizations, messaging someone on LinkedIn, or simply having genuine conversations with people whose work you admire, every interaction has the potential to create unexpected possibilities.

Most importantly: the right people won't just help you find opportunities—they'll remind you that you belong in rooms where you might otherwise feel uncertain.

Before we explore strategic networking approaches, consider your current relationship-building patterns:

- Who is one new person you would like to introduce yourself to this month, and what specifically interests you about their work?

- What opportunity could you create just by starting one meaningful conversation?

- Who do you already know that could help you grow or learn, but you haven't asked for guidance?

- When was the last time you made a genuine professional connection rather than just meeting someone casually?

- What would you want someone to remember about you after a conversation?

- How would you describe who you are and what you're passionate about in 30 seconds?

Now, let's explore how to build the kind of professional relationships that create long-term opportunities.

Mastering Your Professional Introduction

What's an Elevator Pitch?

An elevator pitch is a concise and confident way to introduce yourself and what you care about, highlighting what makes you stand out, in about 30 seconds or less.

Imagine stepping into an elevator with someone you admire— like the CEO of your dream company or a leader from your favorite cause—and having just a few floors to make a lasting impression. That's your moment to shine!

Why It's Important

- It helps you make a strong first impression.

- It builds confidence in how you speak about yourself.

- It can lead to new opportunities—a job, a mentor, or a new friend!

How to Put One Together (Use the "I AM" Method!)

1. I — Introduce Yourself Begin with your name and a brief description of who you are.

"Hi, I'm Maya, a high school student who loves designing eco-friendly fashion."

2. A — Add What You're Passionate About or Good At Share something that makes you stand out—your talents, values, or dreams.

"I'm passionate about using fashion to help the planet."

3. M — Mention Your Goal or What You're Looking For Finish with what you're hoping for—like learning more, finding a mentor, or joining a program.

"I'd love to find opportunities to volunteer or work with people who are also making fashion more sustainable."

Example Elevator Pitch for a Young Woman

Hi, my name is Layla, and I'm a tenth grader who loves robotics and solving problems with technology. I'm a member of my school's robotics team, and we recently won the regional competition! I hope to secure a summer internship or mentorship to gain a deeper understanding of engineering and innovation.

Building Your Strategic Network: Starting Now

Strategic networking isn't something you start when you need a job—it's something you build consistently over time, creating relationships that provide mutual value and support.

There are many ways to start networking:

1. Leverage Your Current Environment Strategically

Your school and community already provide networking opportunities—the key is approaching them with intentional relationship-building in mind.

Strategic school networking:

- Join clubs related to your career interests, not just your hobbies

- Take leadership roles that help you develop relationships with peers and adult advisors

- Attend school-sponsored career events, guest speaker presentations, and industry nights

- Build genuine relationships with teachers who work in or have connections to fields that interest you

Strategic community networking:

- Volunteer for organizations whose missions align with your values and career interests

- Participate in community service projects that connect you with professionals and civic leaders

- Attend local events related to causes or industries you're passionate about

2. Build Your Professional Digital Presence

Creating and developing a LinkedIn profile is essential for modern networking. I strongly recommend you build and perfect your LinkedIn profile and join groups related to your interests.

So why do I recommend LinkedIn?

LinkedIn is a platform for young women (and any young person) seeking internships, not just because it hosts job listings, but because it helps build visibility, credibility, and connections early on. It is also an excellent platform for engaging in discussions and connecting with professionals.

Here's why it's especially powerful:

1. Internship and Entry-Level Job Listings

- LinkedIn has a dedicated Jobs section where students can filter for "Internships" and "Entry-Level" roles by location, industry, and company.

- Many companies specifically post early career programs or high school/college internships on LinkedIn.

2. Visibility to Recruiters

- A polished LinkedIn profile allows recruiters to find you even if you haven't applied.

- Companies increasingly use LinkedIn to search for diverse, up-and-coming talent.

3. Direct Networking

- Students can reach out directly to professionals, alumni, or hiring managers.

- For example:

"Hi Ms. Taylor, I'm a high school junior passionate about environmental science. I saw your post about your work at NOAA and would love to ask for advice on summer internships."

4. Build Confidence & Personal Brand

- Writing a LinkedIn "About" section or listing extracurriculars helps you articulate:
    - Who are you, and what do you stand for?
    - What do you care about?
    - Where do you want to go?

- It reinforces self-advocacy, especially in male-dominated fields like tech, finance, or engineering.

5. Learn from Mentors and Role Models

- By following leaders, companies, or hashtags like #WomenInSTEM or #InternshipOpportunity, you can get:
    - Career insights
    - Scholarship info
    - Motivational stories from other leaders and pioneering trailblazers

6. Digital Portfolio

- A LinkedIn profile acts as a living résumé, where you can showcase:
    - Volunteer work
    - School clubs or leadership roles
    - Certifications or class projects

      ○   Links to writing, websites, or art

Bonus: College and Scholarship Impact

- Some admissions officers and scholarship committees do check applicants' digital footprints. A thoughtful LinkedIn profile can leave a powerful impression.

LinkedIn Age and Preparation Requirements

To create a LinkedIn account, you must be at least 16 years old, as specified in LinkedIn's User Agreement. This age requirement ensures that users have the maturity to engage responsibly on a professional networking platform.

Previously, LinkedIn allowed users as young as 13, but in 2017, the minimum age was raised to 16 to enhance user safety and comply with global privacy standards.

If you're under 16 and interested in preparing for a future LinkedIn presence, consider the following steps:

- **Document Your Achievements**: Keep a record of your volunteer work, school projects, awards, and extracurricular activities. This will make it easier to build a comprehensive profile when you're eligible.

- **Explore Career Interests**: Research various professions and industries to understand the skills and experiences required for each. This can guide your academic and extracurricular choices.

- **Develop Professional Skills**: Focus on building communication, teamwork, and leadership skills through school activities or community involvement.

Once you reach the age of 16, you'll be well-prepared to create a LinkedIn profile that effectively showcases your experiences and aspirations.

Optimizing Your LinkedIn Profile for Maximum Impact

Once you've created your LinkedIn profile, strategic optimization becomes crucial for networking success.

Platforms like LinkedIn aren't just social networks; they're robust career marketplaces where employers and job seekers connect, so getting it right is essential.

Rating your LinkedIn profile involves evaluating various aspects to determine how effectively the profile represents your professional brand and communicates your skills, experience, and value.

LinkedIn Profile Assessment Tool

Use the following rating scale to evaluate each section of your profile. There are 57 points possible. (1 is the low end of the scale)

1. Profile Photo and Banner (1-5 pts)

• Profile Photo: Is it professional, transparent, and high-quality? Does it look approachable and appropriate for your industry?

• Banner Image: Is there a custom banner image that enhances your profile and reflects your brand, interests, or preferred industry?

2. Headline (1-5 pts)

• Is the headline clear and descriptive?

• Does it reflect your title, including key skills or a unique value proposition?

3. Summary (About Section) (1-10 pts)

• Is the summary well-written, engaging, and free of errors?

• Does it provide a concise overview of your background, key achievements, skills, and career goals?

• Does it include relevant keywords for your future career interests or preferred industry?

4. Experience (1-10 pts)

• Are your job titles clear and accurately reflect the roles?

• Does your experience showcase each role's key responsibilities, achievements, and impact?

• Does the experience section demonstrate clear progression?

5. Skills and Endorsements (1-5 pts)

• Are the relevant skills listed and endorsed by your network, manager, or even your teachers? (Work to get at least eight endorsements per skill.)

• Do the skills align with your future career interests, goals, and preferred industry?

6. Recommendations (1-5 pts)

• Do you have recommendations from peers, teachers, colleagues, or managers?

• Are the recommendations detailed, and do they provide insight into your abilities and character?

• Have you given recommendations to others, showing that you are engaged and supportive in your network?

7. Accomplishments (1-5 pts)

• Are relevant accomplishments listed, such as certifications, blogs, papers, projects, honors, and awards?

• Do these accomplishments add value to your profile and demonstrate expertise in your field?

8. Education (1-5 pts)

• Is the education section complete, listing all relevant degrees, institutions, and dates of completion?

• Are any honors or distinctions mentioned?

9. Engagement and Activity (1-5 pts)

• Are you active on LinkedIn, do you share industry-relevant content, post updates, and engage with your network?

• Are you participating in LinkedIn groups or discussions relevant to your industry?

10. Custom URL (1-2 pts)

• Have you customized your LinkedIn profile URL to make it more professional and easier to share?

Interpretation:

Excellent (50-57): The profile is outstanding and well-optimized.

Good (40-49): The profile is strong, but it could be improved.

Average (30-39): The profile is adequate but needs enhancement in several areas.

Below Average (20-29): The profile needs significant improvement in many areas.

Poor (0-19): The profile lacks essential components and needs substantial work.

So, unless you score 57, you have some work to do. Building a standout LinkedIn profile will help you stand out and optimize visibility!

I strongly suggest you use this structured approach to ensure a comprehensive and objective evaluation of your profile.

LinkedIn Profile Enhancement Strategies

A. Compelling Headline

• Craft a headline that goes beyond your job title. Use it to highlight your key skills or a unique selling point. For example, "Digital Marketing Specialist | Helping Brands Grow with Data-Driven Strategies."

B. Professional Photo

- Use a high-quality, professional photo. Ensure you are dressed appropriately and that the background is clean and non-distracting.

C. Engaging Summary

- Write a summary that tells your professional story. Focus on your achievements, skills, volunteer work, specific classes, areas of passion, and accomplishments, as well as what makes you unique. Use first-person pronouns and keep your writing concise, yet informative.

D. Detailed Experience

List any work-related experience, even if it was just an internship, summer job, or volunteer work, providing detailed descriptions of your roles and achievements. Use bullet points for readability and highlight quantifiable achievements. If you have any specific numbers or percentages, please include them. For example:

If you worked in marketing/social media:

- Helped grow Instagram followers by sharing creative posts and stories.

- Created content that led to more people visiting the company's website.

- Suggested ideas that were used in a campaign and helped boost online engagement.

If you helped with events or outreach:

- Helped organize a community event that brought in more customers.

- Reached out to local schools to tell them about our product or service.

- Welcomed visitors, answered questions, and encouraged them to come back.

If you supported a sales team:

- Updated the sales spreadsheet to track customer orders.

- Took notes during sales calls and followed up with clients via email.

- Suggested changes to the brochure to make it easier to understand.

E. Skills and Endorsements

- Add relevant skills to your profile. Aim for a mix of hard and soft skills. You may need to encourage those you have worked with to endorse your skills, whether in a school organization, a job, an internship, or as a volunteer.

Add Skills That Speak — With Heart and Hustle

Your LinkedIn profile isn't just a digital résumé—it's your professional showcase and invitation to opportunities. The Skills section requires strategic curation because LinkedIn only allows you to select from predetermined options, but you can maximize its impact through smart selection and active endorsement building.

You want a mix of hard skills (technical capabilities) and soft skills (behavioral strengths). Together, they convey to potential employers that you're both capable and coachable, skilled and self-aware.

Important LinkedIn Skills functionality:

- Skills are selected from LinkedIn's dropdown menu—you can't write custom descriptions

- You can designate where you used each skill (specific job, project, or school experience)

- Skills appear in your connections' feeds when you add new ones, creating endorsement opportunities

148

- Aim for at least 8 endorsements per skill within a month of adding it—if you don't reach this threshold, consider removing that skill from your profile

Hard Skills = Tools & Techniques

These are the skills you can test or be certified in—they're specific, technical, and tied to the job.

Examples:

- Microsoft Excel
- Canva or Adobe Photoshop
- Google Workspace
- Data entry
- Social media marketing
- Coding (HTML, Python)
- Writing/editing
- Event planning
- Customer service
- Cash handling

Even if you learned them through school projects, a part-time job, or volunteering, they count.

Soft Skills = Behaviors & Attitudes

These are your innate behaviors—the way you think, communicate, and lead. They're harder to measure, but easier to feel.

Examples:

- Reliable
- Curious
- Empathetic

- Team player

- Great communicator

- Self-starter

- Problem-solver

- Positive attitude

- Adaptable under pressure

- Willing to learn

Add 5–10 Skills to Your LinkedIn Profile:

Mix it up! Think:

- 3–5 hard skills from school, jobs, or volunteering

- 2–3 soft skills you know you bring to the table

- 1–2 that are aspirational — qualities you're working on and proud to be growing

Professional Development Tip:

If you're not sure which soft skills to include, ask a teacher, mentor, or friend:

"What's one thing you always notice about how I work with others?"

That answer is probably a skill—and it's worth sharing.

A. Recommendations

- Request recommendations from your manager at your internship, a teacher who gave you an A+ on a project, or the mother of the person you babysat over the summer. Personal testimonials can significantly enhance the credibility of your profile.

B. Showcase projects and any papers or articles you wrote.

- Add any notable work. This can include links to articles you've written, presentations, or project portfolios.

C. Custom URL

- Customize your LinkedIn URL to make it more professional and easier to share (e.g., linkedin.com/in/your name).

D. Engage with Content

- Post and share relevant content. Comment on news relevant to your area of interest, write articles or blogs, and participate in group discussions. This increases your visibility and establishes you as a thought leader.

E. Education and Certifications

- List your educational background and any certifications or courses relevant to your fields of interest. This demonstrates your commitment to continuous learning.

F. Volunteer Experience

- Include volunteer work or extracurricular activities. This can showcase your values and interests outside of school and work.

G. Optimized for Keywords

- Use industry-specific keywords throughout your profile. This helps you get found by recruiters and others searching for your skill set.

H. Consistent Updates

- Regularly update your profile to reflect new roles, skills, and accomplishments. A frequently updated profile signals active engagement and professionalism.

By following these steps, you can create a LinkedIn profile that stands out and effectively communicates your professional brand and value.

Maintaining Your Professional Digital Presence

TIPS FOR MAINTAINING YOUR POSITIVE DIGITAL FOOTPRINT:

Engage Positively: Interact positively and constructively in online discussions and forums.

Monitor Your Presence: Regularly search your name online to monitor your digital footprint and address any inaccurate or harmful information.

Be Mindful of Privacy: Adjust your social media privacy settings to control who can view your personal information and posts.

Maintain Professional Conduct: Always maintain professionalism in all your online interactions, even on personal social media accounts.

Strategic Social Media Networking

X, TikTok, and Instagram: Networking isn't just for adults in blazers swapping business cards—it can (and should!) start while you're still in high school. Platforms like TikTok, Instagram, and X (formerly Twitter) aren't just for trends and memes—they're full of honest conversations led by creators, activists, and industry leaders who are sharing what they know and love. Whether you're into fashion, sports, coding, mental health, or social justice, chances are there's a community talking about it. When you follow those voices, comment thoughtfully, or post about your own interests and school projects. You're not just scrolling, you're building connections. Using your voice online to engage in relevant conversations, share ideas, or even react to current events is a form of modern networking. And the best part? It's fun, informal, and full of opportunities to grow your confidence while learning from people already doing what inspires you.

Starter Actions: How to Begin Networking on Social Media

1. **Follow three people in your dream field** — These could be authors, athletes, entrepreneurs, designers, or activists who share behind-the-scenes insights or advice.

2. **Comment with intention** — Instead of just liking a post, leave a thoughtful comment or question. It shows you're paying attention and want to learn.

3. **Share your ideas or projects** — Whether it's a class project, a community event, or something you made, post it with a short caption explaining why it matters to you.

4. **Join or start a conversation on X** — Look for hashtags around topics you care about (like #WomenInSTEM or #TeenEntrepreneur) and contribute your thoughts.

5. **Reach out with curiosity** — If someone posts something inspiring, send a quick message or reply asking a question or thanking them for sharing; it can lead to a genuine connection.

You don't have to wait until you have an impressive job title to start showing up like a leader. Use your voice now, the right people are already listening!

Expanding Your Network Beyond Digital Platforms

Other ways to expand your network:

1. Attend Strategic Events and Learning Opportunities

Local Events: Attend local workshops, seminars, and networking events with clear professional development goals. Schools often have career days or alumni events that provide excellent networking opportunities.

Online Webinars: Participate in online webinars and virtual events related to your career interests. These are accessible, often free, and allow you to connect with professionals globally.

2. Develop Strategic Mentoring Relationships

School-Based Mentors: Ask teachers or counselors for mentorship or advice on connecting with professionals in your field of interest. Build relationships with adults who can provide guidance and introductions.

Professional Organization Mentorship: Many professional organizations have formal mentorship programs designed specifically for young people entering their fields.

3. Build Your Professional Brand Through Content Creation

Create Valuable Content: Start a blog, YouTube channel, or podcast to share your interests, projects, and insights. This positions you as someone who thinks critically about your field and attracts like-minded professionals.

Showcase Your Skills: Use platforms like GitHub for coding projects, Behance for creative portfolios, or Medium for writing samples to demonstrate your capabilities to potential connections.

The Strategic Value of Professional Networking

Understanding why networking matters helps you approach it strategically rather than randomly:

Opportunity Creation: Networking opens doors to internships, job opportunities, and collaborations that you never would have discovered through traditional job searching alone.

Knowledge and Insight Access: It enables the exchange of ideas, advice, and industry knowledge that accelerates your professional development.

Professional Support System: Building a network provides both emotional and professional support during career transitions, challenges, and growth opportunities.

Industry Visibility: Networking enhances your visibility within your chosen field, making it easier to stay informed about trends, opportunities, and best practices.

Understanding the Six Degrees of Separation

The concept of Six Degrees of Separation suggests that two people on Earth are only six or fewer social connections apart. This means you can connect with anyone through a chain of six people or fewer. Here's how it works:

1. Immediate Circle: Your direct friends, family, and acquaintances.

2. Second Degree: Friends of your friends.

3. Third Degree: Friends of your second-degree connections.

4. Fourth Degree: Friends of your third-degree connections.

5. Fifth Degree: Friends of your fourth-degree connections.

6. Sixth Degree: Friends of your fifth-degree connections, reaching almost anyone globally.

Understanding this principle allows a young woman to realize that even distant connections can be valuable. Reaching out to someone in your immediate circle can lead to introductions to others, exponentially expanding your network. Networking is essential because it leverages this interconnectedness to create opportunities, share knowledge, and build a supportive community.

A Story of Strategic Networking in Action

When Networking Made the Difference

Emma sat across from her counselor, expecting a typical check-in about classes and graduation requirements. Instead, her counselor glanced at the computer, then looked up with a smile.

"Emma, did you know you already have enough credits to graduate? You can actually walk next month."

Emma's heart skipped. Graduate? Next month? She felt a surge of excitement—followed almost immediately by dread. Her thoughts spun: *One month? How will I find a job? My résumé isn't ready. I'm not ready.*

For a moment, panic threatened to overwhelm her. But then she remembered something her mother had told her over and over: "Your network is your safety net. Build it before you need it."

Emma took a deep breath. She had spent years nurturing relationships—checking in with old coaches, keeping up with professors, staying connected with colleagues from her internships. This was the moment to lean into those relationships.

That afternoon, instead of spiraling into anxiety, she made a strategic plan. She called a trusted professor and asked for résumé feedback. She emailed her internship supervisor, letting him know she was graduating early and was eager to bring value to a team. She reached out to friends and mentors, not just asking for help, but sharing clearly how her skills could contribute to their organizations.

The responses came quickly. Encouragement. Referrals. Introductions. Within days, people were passing along opportunities that matched her interests and capabilities. And within weeks, Emma had three job offers in hand—two directly through her network.

The lesson became crystal clear: networking wasn't about schmoozing or collecting business cards. It was about building genuine relationships grounded in trust and reciprocity. Because she had invested time in her network long before she needed it, her network was ready to lift her up when the unexpected arrived.

Here's the truth: when a deadline looms, or life throws you a curveball, you don't want to start networking from scratch. You want to be able to do what Emma did—take a breath, reach out, and trust that the relationships you've built will show up for you.

Emma's experience illustrates something crucial about strategic networking: it's most effective when you invest in relationships before you desperately need them, not when you're facing a crisis.

Your Strategic Networking Journey Starts Now

Effective networking isn't about collecting contacts—it's about building mutually beneficial relationships with people who can support your growth while you contribute value to theirs.

The networking habits you develop now—introducing yourself confidently, following up meaningfully, maintaining relationships consistently—will create compound advantages throughout your career.

Every person you meet thoughtfully, every genuine connection you nurture, every time you offer help before asking for it, you're building a foundation of professional relationships that will support your ambitions for decades.

Your network becomes your net worth, but more than that—it becomes your support system, your learning community, and your opportunity pipeline.

Start where you are. Use what you have. Connect authentically. The professionals you admire today were once beginners too, and many of them remember what it felt like to be where you are now.

The world needs young women who understand that success is collaborative, not competitive. It needs women who build bridges rather than barriers, who lift others while climbing themselves.

Your networking journey starts with your next conversation, your next LinkedIn connection, your next genuine interest in someone else's professional story.

Because when you invest in relationships strategically, opportunities don't just happen to you—they seek you out.

The room you're meant to be in is waiting for you to introduce yourself.

Chapter 11
The Power of Continuous Learning

In today's rapidly evolving professional landscape, your formal education represents just the beginning of your learning journey, not the conclusion. The most successful professionals understand that their degree is a foundation, not a destination—and that continuous learning becomes the bridge between where you are and where you want to be.

The professionals who thrive long-term aren't necessarily those with the highest GPAs or most prestigious degrees—they're the ones who consistently invest in expanding their capabilities, staying curious about emerging trends, and adapting to changes before those changes become requirements.

Story: Kiara Said "Yes" to Growth

Kiara was already skilled at social media management and had been successfully running campaigns for local businesses throughout college. She could have stopped there—her current skills were paying the bills and her clients were satisfied.

But Kiara understood something crucial about professional growth: being good at what exists today doesn't guarantee success with what's coming tomorrow.

When she saw an online course in digital marketing analytics, she didn't dismiss it because she was already "successful." Instead, she recognized an opportunity to deepen her expertise and expand her capabilities. The course covered advanced data visualization, customer journey mapping, and predictive analytics—skills that seemed adjacent to her current work but not immediately necessary.

That strategic learning investment changed everything.

Within six months, those new analytics skills opened doors to freelance opportunities with larger companies who needed someone who could not only create social media campaigns but also measure their ROI and optimize performance based on data insights. The additional capabilities didn't just make her better at her existing work—they positioned her for opportunities she hadn't even known existed.

That one decision to expand beyond her comfort zone transformed her from a competent social media manager into a sought-after digital marketing strategist, commanding higher rates and working with clients who valued strategic thinking alongside creative execution.

Stay curious. Stay ready. Stay one step ahead of what the market needs.

Before we explore strategic approaches to continuous learning, consider your current learning patterns:

- What is one skill you would love to develop that would directly advance your career goals?

- How could you realistically invest time in improving that skill within the next six months?

- What's something meaningful you've learned in the last three months, and how has it impacted your thinking?

- When have you resisted learning opportunities, and what fears or assumptions held you back?

- What capability do you secretly wish you possessed, and what's stopping you from developing it?

Now, let's explore how to build learning habits that create long-term career advantages.

Why Continuous Learning Is Your Career Insurance Policy

Continuous learning involves constantly developing new skills and knowledge throughout your life, but more than that—it's about staying professionally relevant in a world where industries transform faster than traditional education can keep pace.

The professionals who thrive long-term aren't necessarily the smartest or most talented—they're the ones who consistently invest in expanding their capabilities before they need them. They stay curious, seek out new knowledge, join workshops, and read widely because they understand that continuous learning is what keeps you competitive and adaptable in a rapidly changing professional landscape.

For young women building careers, continuous learning becomes even more critical because it provides the credibility and capabilities needed to overcome biases and secure opportunities in competitive environments.

Before we explore strategic approaches to continuous learning, consider your current learning patterns:

- What is one skill you would love to develop that would directly advance your career goals?

- How could you realistically invest time in improving that skill within the next six months?

- What's something meaningful you've learned in the last three months, and how has it impacted your thinking?

- When have you resisted learning opportunities, and what fears or assumptions held you back?

- What capability do you secretly wish you possessed, and what's stopping you from developing it?

Now, let's explore how to build learning habits that create long-term career advantages.

The Strategic Value of Lifelong Learning

This approach is crucial for several reasons:

1. Professional Adaptability in Volatile Markets

Industries and job markets are evolving at unprecedented speed. Staying current with emerging trends, technologies, and methodologies enables you to adapt effectively to changes rather than being displaced by them.

2. Competitive Differentiation Through Proactive Development

Keeping your skills current makes you more competitive, but more importantly, it makes you indispensable. Employers increasingly value individuals who proactively seek to enhance their capabilities rather than waiting for training to be provided.

3. Innovation Through Cross-Disciplinary Knowledge

Continuous learning fosters creativity and innovation by exposing you to diverse perspectives and methodologies. It helps you think critically and solve problems more effectively by drawing connections across different fields and approaches.

4. Confidence Building Through Competence Development

Learning new capabilities contributes to deep personal satisfaction and professional confidence. When you can handle challenges that previously seemed intimidating, your overall motivation and self-efficacy increase significantly.

5. Opportunity Creation Through Skill Expansion

Advanced skills and knowledge don't just open existing career opportunities—they create new ones. When you develop capabilities that are in demand but short supply, you become someone who can write their own career path.

Unique Advantages for Women Early in Their Careers

For women building careers, continuous learning provides specific advantages for navigating challenges and securing opportunities:

Confidence Building Through Demonstrated Competence

Acquiring new skills and knowledge builds genuine confidence based on actual capability rather than empty affirmations. When you can confidently discuss emerging industry trends or apply new technologies, your credibility in professional conversations increases dramatically.

Bias Mitigation Through Expertise Development

While bias remains a challenge, continuous learning provides you with the expertise and credibility to overcome stereotypes. When your knowledge and capabilities are clearly superior, it becomes much harder for others to dismiss your contributions or question your competence.

Network Expansion Through Learning Communities

Learning environments—whether formal courses, conferences, or online communities—provide natural networking opportunities with industry professionals, mentors, and peers who share your commitment to growth.

Strategic Versatility Through Cross-Functional Skills

Developing diverse capabilities makes you more versatile and valuable to employers, but it also gives you more career options and negotiating power. When you can contribute across multiple areas, you become less vulnerable to industry downturns or organizational changes.

Leadership Preparation Through Intentional Development

Continuous learning in leadership, communication, and strategic thinking prepares you for advancement opportunities. When leadership positions open, you'll already have the capabilities needed rather than hoping to learn them on the job.

How Strategic Learning Creates Professional Differentiation

Strategic continuous learning creates specific competitive advantages:

Initiative Demonstration Through Self-Directed Growth

Continuous learners signal to employers that they are proactive about their career development, self-motivated, and committed to professional excellence. This initiative often matters more than current skill level for advancement decisions.

Comprehensive Capability Portfolio

A broad and current skill set makes you attractive for both promotions and new opportunities, but more importantly, it gives you options. When you're not dependent on a single skill set, you have more freedom to pursue opportunities that align with your goals.

Enhanced Problem-Solving Through Diverse Knowledge

Continuous learners are often superior problem solvers because they can draw from a wide array of knowledge and methodologies when facing challenges. This ability to synthesize solutions from multiple disciplines becomes increasingly valuable at higher levels.

Change Resilience Through Learning Agility

Employers increasingly value employees who can quickly adapt to new technologies, processes, and market conditions. When you've demonstrated ability to master new capabilities efficiently, you become a more resilient and reliable asset during periods of change.

Thought Leadership Through Knowledge Sharing

By staying informed about industry developments and sharing insights, you can establish yourself as a thought leader in your field. This enhances your professional reputation and creates opportunities for speaking, writing, and consulting.

Long-Term Career Security Through Relevance Maintenance

Continuous learning contributes to long-term career success by ensuring your capabilities remain relevant and valuable even as markets evolve. This is the closest thing to job security in an unpredictable economy.

A Personal Story of Learning as Career Transformation

Learning Without Borders

From a young age, I have had a deep passion for travel. I wanted to explore the world, not just as a tourist, but in a way that truly allowed me to understand different people, cultures, and perspectives. I knew that if I wanted to work internationally one day, I'd need more than just a passport. I needed to learn how to connect.

So, while I was in university, I chose to study French. Eventually, I earned a minor in it, and for my final semester, I studied abroad in France at the Alliance Française. That experience changed everything. I worked on a project exploring cultural differences between France and the United States. With every interaction and conversation, I felt a new world opening up to me because I could finally speak the language.

That was just the beginning.

Next came Spanish. Then Chinese. And now, I'm learning Italian.

Each new language brought more than vocabulary—confidence, global awareness, and opportunity. Being multilingual became a key that unlocked jobs, connections, and incredible adventures I would have never imagined.

Continuous learning didn't just enrich my life—it shaped my entire career.

And here's what I've learned: You don't need to master everything at once. Just stay curious. Be willing to be a beginner. Whether it's learning a language, a skill, a sport, or a new technology, what you invest in yourself always comes back in unexpected, powerful ways.

This story illustrates something crucial about strategic learning: the capabilities you develop often create opportunities you never expected. Each language I learned opened doors I hadn't even known existed.

Building Your Strategic Learning Framework

Effective continuous learning isn't about randomly collecting skills—it's about strategically building capabilities that compound over time to create unique professional advantages.

Identify High-Impact Learning Opportunities

Focus your learning investments on capabilities that:

- Are increasingly in demand within your industry

- Complement your existing strengths to create unique capability combinations

- Transfer across multiple roles and industries

- Position you ahead of trends rather than following them

Create Learning Systems, Not Just Learning Goals

Instead of setting vague learning goals, build sustainable systems:

- Dedicate specific time blocks to learning activities

- Join communities or groups focused on areas you want to develop

- Find accountability partners who share your commitment to growth

- Document and apply what you learn to reinforce retention

Balance Depth with Breadth

Strategic learners develop:

- Deep expertise in their core professional area

- Complementary skills that enhance their primary capabilities

- Broad knowledge that helps them spot connections and opportunities

- Meta-learning skills that help them acquire new capabilities efficiently

Leverage Modern Learning Resources

Take advantage of accessible learning options:

- Online courses and certifications for technical skills

- Industry conferences and workshops for networking and trend awareness

- Professional books and podcasts for deep insights

- Mentorship relationships for practical guidance

- Cross-functional projects for hands-on experience

Your Continuous Learning Journey Starts Now

Strategic continuous learning isn't just about staying current—it's about staying ahead. It's about building capabilities before you need them, spotting opportunities before they become obvious, and developing the adaptability to thrive regardless of how your industry evolves.

The learning investments you make now—whether technical skills, languages, leadership capabilities, or industry knowledge—compound over time to create unique professional advantages that can't be replicated quickly.

Every course you complete, every book you read thoughtfully, every skill you develop deliberately, you're building a foundation of capabilities that will support your ambitions throughout your career.

The professionals who succeed long-term aren't the ones who know the most right now—they're the ones who learn the fastest and most strategically.

Your learning journey isn't just about acquiring knowledge—it's about developing the confidence to tackle challenges you've never faced, the curiosity to explore possibilities you hadn't considered, and the adaptability to thrive in careers that don't even exist yet.

Stay curious. Stay ready. But most importantly, stay strategic about what you choose to learn and why.

The world needs women who combine deep expertise with broad curiosity, who can bridge disciplines and cultures, who never stop growing.

Your next learning opportunity is waiting. What will you choose to master?

Because in a world of constant change, your ability to learn isn't just an advantage—it's your insurance policy for a career without limits.

Chapter 12
Strategic Self-Care for
Sustainable Success

Self-care isn't about bubble baths and spa days—it's about building the physical, mental, and emotional resilience needed to sustain high performance over decades, not just months. The most successful professionals understand that taking care of themselves isn't selfish; it's strategic. It's how you maintain the energy, creativity, and resilience needed to achieve long-term goals rather than just short-term wins.

Story: Leah Chose Herself First

Leah had always been the "yes" person in her friend group. Coffee dates she didn't really want? Yes. Volunteering for extra projects at work when she was already overwhelmed? Yes. Staying up late scrolling social media even when she knew she needed sleep? Always yes.

She thought being available and agreeable was part of being a supportive friend and dedicated professional. But by her senior year of college, Leah was exhausted, scattered, and increasingly resentful of commitments that had once felt manageable.

The turning point came during what should have been a relaxing weekend. She had agreed to three different social obligations, spent hours comparing her life to others' highlight reels on Instagram, and ended Sunday night feeling more drained than when the weekend began.

That's when Leah made a strategic decision: she would start protecting her energy the same way she protected her money—by being intentional about where she invested it.

When Leah started saying "no" to things that drained her energy, she found she had more space for things that actually mattered. That shift didn't just give her more peace—it gave her back time, focus, and a sense of direction she hadn't felt in months.

Instead of defaulting to yet another coffee date she didn't want, she used that hour to volunteer at a food bank that aligned with her values. Instead of mindlessly scrolling social media, she polished her LinkedIn profile and drafted a pitch for a passion project. Instead of saying yes to every social invitation, she chose the ones where she could genuinely connect with people who energized rather than drained her.

Little by little, those intentional choices started to compound— into confidence, clarity, and a profound sense of agency over her own life.

Leah learned that sometimes the most significant energy drain doesn't come from other people; it comes from the pressure to stay constantly plugged in and available. The endless social media scrolling, the compulsive comparison to others' curated lives, the need to respond immediately to every notification—all of it was leaving her emotionally exhausted without her even realizing it.

She discovered that real self-care isn't just spa treatments and bubble baths. It's knowing when to log off, when to say no, and when to make space for activities that genuinely fill you up instead of wearing you down. It's understanding that pride comes from being intentional about your choices.

Most importantly, Leah learned that you don't owe your time or energy to everything and everyone—just to what moves you forward and aligns with your values.

Protecting your energy isn't selfish. It's a form of self-respect, and it's essential for sustainable success.

Why Strategic Self-Care Is Your Professional Superpower

Self-care isn't about weekly manicures and massage treatments—it's about building the physical, mental, and emotional resilience needed to sustain high performance over decades, not just months.

Authentic self-care means listening to your body, protecting your energy, and showing yourself the same strategic care you would show a valuable business asset. Because that's exactly what you are. It includes getting adequate sleep, eating well, and moving your body, but it also means knowing when to rest, when to say "no," and when to ask for help.

It's about checking in with your emotions, managing stress constructively, and giving yourself permission to feel everything without judgment while still maintaining professional effectiveness.

Most importantly: physical, mental, and emotional self-care are interconnected. When you take care of yourself strategically, you demonstrate to the world—and to yourself—that you understand your own value and are committed to protecting your long-term capabilities.

Before we explore strategic self-care approaches, honestly assess your current patterns:

- Where in your life are you saying "yes" when you should say "no" to protect your capacity for priorities that matter?

- What's one specific action you could take this week to recharge your mind, body, or emotional resilience?

- Where do you consistently feel drained, and what systemic changes need to happen?

- What boundaries have you been afraid to set, and what's the real cost of not setting them?

- What activities genuinely bring you peace and energy, and how often do you actually prioritize them?

Now, let's explore how to build self-care systems that support long-term success rather than just providing temporary relief.

The Professional Case for Strategic Self-Care

Self-care is crucial for well-being and success, especially for young women embarking on their professional journeys. Prioritizing self-care is essential for several reasons:

Burnout Prevention Through Sustainable Practices

Starting a career can be demanding, and neglecting self-care leads to physical and mental exhaustion that reduces both productivity and job satisfaction. More importantly, burnout can derail careers for months or years, making prevention far more strategic than recovery.

Performance Enhancement Through Strategic Recovery

Effective self-care practices improve focus, creativity, and problem-solving abilities, directly impacting professional performance. Well-rested, healthy professionals consistently outperform exhausted ones, even when the exhausted ones work longer hours.

Resilience Building for Long-Term Success

Strategic self-care builds resilience against stress and setbacks, which are inevitable in any ambitious career. Resilient professionals recover faster from challenges and maintain perspective during difficult periods.

Health as Professional Infrastructure

Physical and mental health are foundational infrastructure for sustaining career growth. Poor health doesn't just affect quality of life—it limits career opportunities, reduces earning potential, and can derail long-term goals.

Sustainable Integration Rather Than Perfect Balance

Early-career professionals often struggle with work-life integration (balance being somewhat unrealistic in demanding careers). Strategic self-care helps create boundaries and promotes sustainable integration between professional ambitions and personal well-being.

Strategic Self-Care Framework for Young Women

Effective self-care isn't random acts of kindness to yourself— it's a systematic approach to maintaining your capacity for excellence:

1. Physical Foundation Building

Your body is your most important business asset—treat it accordingly:

Strategic Exercise: Engage in activities that boost energy, improve mood, and enhance overall health. Choose activities you actually enjoy rather than forcing yourself through exercise you hate.

Nutritional Excellence: Maintain a balanced diet rich in nutrients that support cognitive function and physical stamina. Proper nutrition isn't about perfection—it's about consistency and energy optimization.

Sleep as Performance Enhancement: Aim for 7-9 hours of quality sleep per night. Sleep is crucial for cognitive function, emotional regulation, and immune system health. Treat sleep as non-negotiable professional preparation.

Preventive Health Care: Regular medical, gynecological, and dental check-ups address potential issues before they become career-limiting problems.

Energy Management Through Relationship Curation: I have a simple framework for managing relationships based on their energy impact:

Red Zone People: These individuals consistently drain your energy and offer little in return. They create unnecessary stress and drama. While some stress is inevitable in ambitious careers, you don't need to add relationship stress to the mix.

Orange Zone People: People you must interact with professionally or through family obligations, but who don't actively support your growth. Set clear boundaries and limit unnecessary engagement.

Green Zone People: These individuals genuinely care about your success and well-being without expecting anything in return. Invest your relationship energy here.

Quick Stress Management Tool: When you feel overwhelmed, take three deep, intentional breaths. This simple technique calms your nervous system, clears your mind, and gives you space to respond thoughtfully rather than react impulsively.

2. Emotional Resilience Development

Emotional self-care builds the psychological foundation for handling career challenges:

Mindfulness and Meditation: Regular mindfulness practices help manage stress and enhance emotional regulation. Even five minutes daily can improve your ability to stay calm under pressure.

Emotional Processing: Journaling, talking to trusted friends, or working with a therapist helps process emotions constructively. Don't let stress accumulate without release.

Boundary Setting: Learn to say "no" strategically to prevent overcommitting. Every yes to something unimportant is a no to something that matters more.

3. Cognitive Optimization

Mental self-care maintains and enhances your thinking capabilities:

Strategic Learning: Engage in activities that stimulate your mind while advancing your goals—reading industry publications, learning new skills, or solving complex problems.

Productive Breaks: Regular breaks during work prevent mental fatigue and actually improve productivity. Your brain needs recovery time to maintain peak performance.

Restorative Activities: Engage in hobbies that bring genuine joy and relaxation. Activities unrelated to work help prevent mental tunnel vision and restore creativity.

4. Social Support Systems

Strategic relationship building provides essential support for career challenges:

Professional Support Networks: Maintain connections with mentors, colleagues, and industry peers who can provide guidance, opportunities, and perspective.

Personal Support Systems: Nurture relationships with friends and family who support your ambitions and provide emotional grounding outside of work.

Community Engagement: Participate in activities that connect you with like-minded people who share your values and interests.

5. Professional Sustainability Practices

Professional self-care ensures long-term career viability:

Mentorship Relationships: Develop relationships with mentors who can provide guidance, support, and perspective on career challenges. Mentorship accelerates learning and reduces isolation.

Strategic Time Management: Prioritize tasks based on impact, delegate when possible, and use tools to manage your time efficiently. Effective time management reduces stress and increases meaningful productivity.

Integration Over Balance: Rather than perfect work-life balance, aim for sustainable integration that allows you to excel professionally while maintaining personal well-being.

The Success Connection: Why Self-Care Drives Performance

Strategic self-care directly impacts professional performance:

Sustained Energy Management: Physical self-care ensures you have the energy and stamina to meet job demands consistently, not just during crisis periods.

Enhanced Cognitive Performance: Mental self-care improves focus, decision-making, and creative problem-solving—capabilities that become more valuable at higher career levels.

Emotional Intelligence and Stability: Emotional self-care helps you manage stress and maintain perspective, which is essential for leadership and collaborative success.

Integrated Well-Being: When physical, emotional, and mental self-care work together, they create the foundation for sustained high performance and long-term career satisfaction.

A Story of Self-Care as Career Strategy

Annie's Story: Choosing Self-Care Every Day

Annie always loved staying active. She was a student athlete who gave her all in every game. She loved the energy, the teamwork, and the thrill of competition. Back then, she thought self-care meant working hard, staying fit, and eating healthy snacks.

But one week, everything changed.

"I had crushed it," Annie remembers. "I hit my sales goals, worked out every morning, and even stuck to my clean eating plan. But by Friday, I felt ... awful. My chest was tight, I couldn't stop overthinking everything, and I burst into tears when I lost my phone for five minutes. That's when it hit me—I had done everything *right* physically but completely ignored my mind and soul."

177

That moment helped Annie realize self-care isn't just about movement and discipline—it's also about *slowing down, tuning in*, and *showing yourself grace.*

Now, Annie makes time for things that refill her inner cup. She reads books that help her grow, listens to inspiring podcasts, journals her thoughts, and spends time in nature to reconnect with her inner self and with God. She still loves staying active, but now she also knows the power of quiet moments, deep breaths, and daily gratitude.

Sometimes, when she reaches a significant goal, she celebrates by getting her hair done or treating herself to something that brings her joy and confidence. But the most important part? She no longer waits until she's burnt out to care for herself. Self-care is part of her everyday life—a reward and a routine.

"I've battled anxiety and depression before," Annie says. "And I've learned that the mind is the most significant battlefield. You can't pour from an empty cup. So, fill your day with movement, peace, prayer, and purpose."

Her advice to you? Don't wait. Take care of your *whole* self—body, mind, and heart because your health is your greatest treasure. And no amount of success is worth losing yourself over.

Annie's story illustrates something crucial: comprehensive self-care requires attention to all dimensions of well-being—physical, mental, emotional, and spiritual. When any one area is neglected, the entire system becomes vulnerable.

Your Strategic Self-Care Action Plan

Building sustainable self-care requires intentional systems, not just good intentions:

Create Non-Negotiable Self-Care Standards

Identify the minimum self-care practices you need to maintain baseline performance:

- Minimum sleep requirements for cognitive function

- Exercise frequency needed for energy and stress management
- Social connection time required for emotional well-being
- Recovery activities that restore your mental capacity

Build Self-Care Into Your Schedule

Treat self-care like any other important appointment:

- Schedule exercise sessions and protect them like client meetings
- Block time for meal preparation and mindful eating
- Set boundaries around work hours to ensure adequate rest
- Plan recovery activities after high-stress periods

Develop Early Warning Systems

Recognize signs that your self-care needs adjustment:

- Physical symptoms like headaches, fatigue, or frequent illness
- Emotional indicators like irritability, anxiety, or feeling overwhelmed
- Cognitive changes like difficulty focusing or making decisions
- Relationship impacts like withdrawing from others or increased conflict

Create Support Systems for Accountability

Build networks that support your self-care commitments:

- Find workout partners or accountability buddies
- Join groups focused on professional wellness
- Work with mentors who model sustainable success

- Communicate your boundaries clearly to colleagues and family

Your Self-Care Legacy Starts Now

Strategic self-care isn't just about feeling good—it's about building the foundation for sustained excellence throughout your career. When you take care of yourself systematically, you demonstrate to the world and to yourself that you understand your own value and are committed to protecting your long-term capabilities.

The most successful women I know aren't the ones who sacrifice their well-being for short-term achievements—they're the ones who build self-care systems that support their ambitions over decades, not just months.

Every boundary you set, every "no" you say to protect your energy, every investment you make in your physical and mental health, you're building the resilience needed for whatever challenges and opportunities await.

Taking care of yourself isn't selfish—it's strategic. It's how you ensure that you'll have the energy, creativity, and emotional stability needed to achieve your biggest goals while maintaining your health, relationships, and sense of purpose.

The world needs women who can sustain excellence without burning out, who can lead without sacrificing their well-being, who understand that self-care isn't weakness—it's wisdom.

Your self-care journey starts with the next choice you make about how to treat yourself, the next boundary you set, the next time you choose what serves your long-term success over short-term approval.

Because when you take care of yourself strategically, you don't just survive your ambitions—you thrive through them.

Your "Be BAD" Journey Begins

As you finish this book, I want you to picture your career as a castle. A place of strength. A place you've worked hard to build. Every bold step, every ambitious move, every determined push forward has added another stone to your fortress.

But here's the truth: a castle without protection is vulnerable. No matter how tall its walls, without a moat, it can be breached.

Your career moat is what protects everything you've built. It's the layer that ensures your value can't easily be diminished, dismissed, or replaced. Companies have moats—cost advantages, networks, brand power. And so should you.

- When you deliver results consistently, you widen your moat.

- When you invest in relationships, your network strengthens the walls.

- When you build expertise others can't replicate, you raise the drawbridge.

- When you nurture your brand and credibility, your castle shines across the landscape.

- When you own your niche, you become the queen of your domain.

This is the essence of being BAD:

- Bold enough to build a fortress that reflects your worth.

- Ambitious enough to surround it with defenses that grow stronger over time.

- Determined enough to guard it from those who may try to diminish it.

I wrote this book for my daughters, Ashley and Emma. But as I finish these final words, I realize I've also been writing to the version of myself who needed this advice twenty years ago—the young woman who didn't yet know that her ambition wasn't too much, it was exactly enough.

To every reader who's made it this far: you've just invested hours learning strategies for building your career. Now comes the most important part—actually building it.

Your castle awaits. Your moat protects it. And every bold choice, ambitious goal, and determined action becomes another stone in the fortress you're creating.

The women who came before us fought for our right to build. The women who come after us are watching to see what we do with that right.

So step out, Good Girl. Be BAD. Not just for yourself, but for every girl who needs to see that it's possible.

Your kingdom is waiting. And you were born to reign.

www.ingramcontent.com/pod-product-compliance
Lightning Source LLC
Chambersburg PA
CBHW050459190326
41458CB00005B/1351